T0289275

Also by Patrick Barry

Good with Words: Writing and Editing

The Syntax of Sports, Class 1: The Words under the Words

THE Syntax OF Sports

Class 2: The Power of the Particular

Patrick Barry

Published in the United States of America by
Michigan Publishing

DOI: http://dx.doi.org/10.3998/mpub.11567096

ISBN 978-1-60785-593-4 (paper)
ISBN 978-1-60785-594-1 (e-book)
ISBN 978-1-60785-595-8 (OA)

An imprint of Michigan Publishing, Maize Books serves the publishing needs of the University of Michigan community by making high-quality scholarship widely available in print and online. It represents a new model for authors seeking to share their work within and beyond the academy, offering streamlined selection, production, and distribution processes. Maize Books is intended as a complement to more formal modes of publication in a wide range of disciplinary areas.
http://www.maizebooks.org

For my sister Kathleen, whose emails and text messages over the years have been, for me, some of the best—and certainly the funniest—writing around

Whatever I do is about picking examples, because you can't show the whole world. You always have to find the whole in extreme detail.

—Photographer Wolfgang Tillmans, quoted in
"The Life and Art of Wolfgang Tillmans" (2018)

Words are no small things.

—Fredrik Backman, *Beartown* (2016)

Contents

Class Roster

Teacher
Professor Patrick Barry

Student	*Major*
Ms. Amos	Psychology
Ms. Bart	Business
Mr. Boh	Engineering
Ms. Bristol	Kinesiology
Ms. Burke	Political Science
Mr. Carlos	Biochemistry
Ms. Carroll	Math
Ms. Cawlow	Art History
Mr. Dewey	Education
Mr. Farnoff	American Studies
Ms. Franzoni	History
Ms. Henrietta	Communications
Ms. Ida	Communications
Mr. Leigh	Film
Ms. Maat	Biology
Mr. Marshall	Political Science
Ms. Nina	Music
Ms. Toth	English / Creative Writing
Ms. Warsaw	Chemistry / Physics
Mr. Wild	English
Ms. Yona	Comparative Literature

1

The Life of Language

Mr. Dewey: So I'm ready for the James Joyce anecdote.

Prof. Barry: The one about syntax?

Mr. Dewey: Yeah. You said last class that you were intentionally saving it for this class.

Prof. Barry: I said a lot of things last class.

Mr. Dewey: Does that mean you're not going to tell us the anecdote?

Prof. Barry: No. I'm going to tell you the anecdote. But first I want to talk about the word *peruse*.

Mr. Dewey: *Peruse*?

Prof. Barry: Yeah. What do you think it means? If I told you I was perusing an article on ESPN.com, how would you describe what I was doing? Would you say that I was skimming the article or that I was reading it carefully?

Mr. Dewey: I would say you were skimming it.

Prof. Barry: So *peruse* means "to skim"?

Mr. Dewey: Yeah.

Prof. Barry: Anybody want to take a different view?

(*Silence*)

No? Everybody thinks *peruse* means "to skim"? Okay. Well, let's check a dictionary. Here's how the *Merriam-Webster* dictionary defines *peruse*.

Mr. Dewey: "To examine or consider with attention and detail: study."

Prof. Barry: Not exactly "to skim," is it? In fact, "to examine or consider with attention and detail" is pretty much the opposite of "to skim," isn't it?

Mr. Dewey: Yeah.

Prof. Barry: But look closely: that's just the first definition. Now read the second.

Mr. Dewey: "To look over or through in a casual or cursory way."

Prof. Barry: Which is another way of saying?

Mr. Dewey: "To skim."

Prof. Barry: So *peruse* does mean "to skim."

Mr. Dewey: Yeah.

Prof. Barry: And it doesn't mean "to skim."

Mr. Dewey: Right.

Prof. Barry: That's kind of annoying, right—for a word to mean both one thing and the opposite of that thing?

Mr. Dewey: A little, yeah.

Prof. Barry: So perhaps it's also a good reminder of something I often tell my law students, borrowing a bit from a famous

observation made by Supreme Court Justice Oliver Wendell Holmes Jr. back in 1881.

Can you read it off the slide for us, please?

Mr. Dewey: "The life of language has not been logic: it has been experience."

Prof. Barry: Holmes's version, which shows up in his classic book *The Common Law*, is "The life of the law has not been logic: it has been experience."

But I think words like *peruse* show that the same is true of language, particularly the English language. It's not logical that the same word can mean its opposite. That's only something that can happen over time—as language evolves and people use it in different, sometimes contradictory ways.

Or take the example of heteronyms. Those don't seem logical at all.

Mr. Dewey: What are heteronyms?

Prof. Barry: Anybody know? Maybe Mr. Wild, our English major?

Mr. Wild: Aren't heteronyms words that are spelled the same but have different meanings?

Prof. Barry: Yeah, and they have different pronunciations too.

Mr. Wild: Right.

Prof. Barry: Here's one. It appears in a sentence written about the person who helped put Detroit on the musical map: legendary producer Berry Gordy.

Mr. Wild: "Berry Gordy at Motown helped many artists record their first record."

Prof. Barry: See how that works? The words *record* and *record* have the same exact spelling, but they have very different meanings and pronunciations.

Mr. Wild: Right.

Prof. Barry: Or how about this one?

Mr. Wild: "To be successful, the farm needs to produce better produce."

Prof. Barry: And from the world of law, one for Mr. Marshall.

Mr. Marshall: "An advocate needs to advocate."

Prof. Barry: Imagine trying to explain these to people who are learning English as a second language. They'd hate you.

It's not like there is a tidy grammatical principle you can cite to clear up their confusion. There is no rule or prescription that explains what makes one usage different from the other. The plain fact is that with this and many other aspects of language, you can't reason your way to mastery. You have to just trudge along through constant exposure and practice.

Ms. Yona (*jumping in*): I remember reading that there are actually a decent number of heteronyms in German and even more in Dutch.

Prof. Barry: Do either have as many as English does?

Ms. Yona: How many does English have?

Prof. Barry: I think more than three hundred.

Ms. Yona: Then maybe not.

Prof. Barry: Well, it's something to look into. For now, let's check out one more example in English as a way to transition into something we are going to do to start each class. Read it for us, please.

Ms. Yona: "Many television shows use a technique at the beginning of each episode to help present the present episode."

Prof. Barry: You know the technique I'm talking about? It's that short sequence that reminds viewers what happened on earlier episodes. *The Wire* did it. *Game of Thrones* did it. And so, I imagine, will a bunch of hit shows in the future.

Ms. Yona: You mean the recap sequence?

Prof. Barry: Yeah. But what's another term for it?

Ms. Yona: "Previously On"?

Prof. Barry: Right. "Previously On." That's what we're about to do.

2

Previously On

Prof. Barry: Say a bit more about "Previously On," Ms. Yona. What function does it serve? Why do television shows spend time on it?

Ms. Yona: I think because it gives the audience a chance to get ready for the new episode. It provides some really useful—what's the word?

Prof. Barry: *Context*?

Ms. Yona: Yeah. Context. It provides some really useful context.

Prof. Barry: So you're a fan of "Previously On"?

Ms. Yona: Yeah. I often tell my friends to be quiet during it.

Prof. Barry: You want to be able to pay attention, right? So you can figure out what was important from the last episode.

Ms. Yona: Right.

Prof. Barry: Because?

Ms. Yona: Because then I'm more likely to understand the new episode.

Prof. Barry: Which is another way of saying that "Previously On" helps prepare you to absorb new material. It's an aid to comprehension.

Ms. Yona: Yeah.

Prof. Barry: So now apply that to school. How might a teacher use "Previously On" to help her students learn better?

Ms. Yona: She could take some time at the beginning of each class to review key material from the previous classes.

Prof. Barry: Good. Why might that be useful?

Ms. Yona: Because sometimes it can be tough to immediately reconnect with where the class left off, particularly if you haven't had that class in a while.

Prof. Barry: Like with our class.

Ms. Yona: Right. We haven't had class in, what, a week?

Prof. Barry: Yup. Our first session was at this same time a week ago.

Ms. Yona: That can feel like a long time. I definitely don't remember everything we covered in that session.

Prof. Barry: I doubt you're the only one. So to help everyone's brain a bit, what if we start each class with a short review of the previous class, especially if that review makes the overall arc of a course a little clearer—sound good?

Ms. Yona: Yeah. What I like about when TV shows do "Previously On" is that you start to see how various pieces of a larger story fit together.

Prof. Barry: Right. Themes develop. Patterns emerge.

Ms. Yona: Yeah.

Prof. Barry: You think that can also happen with a class?

Ms. Yona: I hope so.

Prof. Barry: Me too. Which is why we're going to do our brand of "Previously On" throughout the semester. We'll start with a little help from a baseball player whose plaque in the Hall of Fame says he hit "almost 800 home runs"—even though he never actually played in the Major Leagues.

3

Josh Gibson

Prof. Barry: To begin our version of "Previously On," Mr. Dewey, please remind everyone of the main writing principle we learned last class. It was a tidy little phrase.

Mr. Dewey: "The words you choose can change the world people see."

Prof. Barry: Right. "The words you choose can change the world people see." We got that from the Nobel Prize–winning psychologist Daniel Kahneman and his example of the different ways to frame the outcome of the 2006 World Cup. If you say "France lost," people may see one version of the match. But if you say "Italy won"?

Mr. Dewey: People see a very different version.

Prof. Barry: Just like if doctors talk in terms of mortality rates, patients react one way. But?

Mr. Dewey: If they talk in terms of survival rates, patients react a different way.

Prof. Barry: Even when the rates are functionally equivalent.

Mr. Dewey: Right.

Prof. Barry: Good. Now let's see if a similar framing effect can be applied to how we characterize people—namely, the baseball player Josh Gibson. Have you ever heard of him?

Mr. Dewey: I don't think so.

Prof. Barry: That's okay. I bet Ms. Bristol, our sports wiz, has. Am I right, Ms. Bristol?

Ms. Bristol: Yeah. I've heard of Josh Gibson.

Prof. Barry: Tell us a little about him.

Ms. Bristol: Didn't he play in the Negro Leagues back before Jackie Robinson integrated Major League Baseball?

Prof. Barry: He did. This was the era of legendary players like Satchel Paige, Oscar Charleston, and Cool Papa Bell. Do you know Gibson's position?

Ms. Bristol: Catcher?

Prof. Barry: Good. There's a neat anecdote about him going to a game between the Homestead Grays and the Kansas City Monarchs as a spectator when he was about eighteen years old, having already developed quite a reputation as a promising prospect. When the Grays' veteran catcher Buck Ewing hurt his hand in an early inning, the team's manager supposedly saw that Gibson was in the stands, walked over to him, and asked if he would take Ewing's place.

Ms. Bristol: What did Gibson say?

Prof. Barry: Not much, I don't think. He was a pretty quiet guy. But according to the story, Gibson walked into the Grays' locker room, put on Ewing's uniform, and started playing catcher for the team. From that point on, Ewing had to find a new gig.

Ms. Bristol: Did that actually happen?

Prof. Barry: Probably not. In *Josh Gibson: The Power and the Darkness*, journalist Mark Ribowsky points to evidence that suggests the story is more myth than reality, but it's still a fun thing to retell.

Even more fun: Gibson's career stats. In addition to hitting nearly 800 home runs, his career batting average was .355. That's only a little behind the all-time record of .366 held by Ty Cobb, who played most of his career here in Michigan.

Ms. Bristol: For the Detroit Tigers, right?

Prof. Barry: Right, but Gibson's .355 average may be even more impressive than Cobb's .366, considering Gibson also hit all those home runs.

Ms. Bristol: How many homes runs did Cobb hit?

Prof. Barry: Only about one hundred. Plus, the kinds of homers Gibson hit were epic. There are accounts of them traveling as far as five or six hundred feet. He is said to be the only player to ever hit a fair ball out of Yankee Stadium.

And even if that story is not actually true, that people believe it *could* be true says a lot about Gibson's almost otherworldly strength.

Ms. Bristol: Right.

Prof. Barry: But my favorite Gibson tale is told by Robert Peterson in his book about the Negro Leagues, *Only the Balls Were White*. Could you start reading it for us, please? During the game Peterson describes, Gibson is playing for the Pittsburgh Crawfords.

Ms. Bristol: "One day during the 1930s the Pittsburgh Crawfords were playing at Forbes Field in Pittsburgh when their young catcher, Josh Gibson, hit the ball so high and far that no one saw it come down. After scanning the sky carefully for a few minutes, the umpire deliberated and ruled it a home run."

Prof. Barry: Isn't that pretty cool? In a battle against gravity—or at least against the umpire's eyesight—Josh Gibson won.

But keep reading, Ms. Bristol. The ending of the story is the best part.

Ms. Bristol: "The next day the Crawfords were playing in Philadelphia when suddenly a ball dropped out of the heavens and was caught by the startled center-fielder on the opposing club. The umpire made the only possible ruling. Pointing to Gibson he shouted, 'Yer out—yesterday, in Pittsburgh!'"

4

The Black Babe Ruth, the Michigan of the East, and the Man Who Accompanied Jacqueline Kennedy to Paris

Prof. Barry: The way Josh Gibson helps us do "Previously On" is by giving us a chance to review some of the work we did last class with word choice and framing. Here, for example, is how many people described Gibson. Please read it for us, Ms. Bristol.

Ms. Bristol: "The black Babe Ruth."

Prof. Barry: And who is Babe Ruth?

Ms. Bristol: Perhaps the best home run hitter of all time.

Prof. Barry: What race was he?

Ms. Bristol: White.

Prof. Barry: So what's the point of the nickname the "black Babe Ruth"? What message is it trying to communicate about Josh Gibson?

Ms. Bristol: It's trying to communicate that Gibson was a really good baseball player, that he was the black version of the best home run hitter of all time.

Prof. Barry: Who is the dominant figure in that comparison? Who holds the more privileged and esteemed position?

Ms. Bristol: Babe Ruth.

Prof. Barry: How so?

Ms. Bristol: Because he's framed as the reference point. He's the standard by which Josh Gibson is judged.

Prof. Barry: But that's not our only option as far as framing goes, right?

Ms. Bristol: Right.

Prof. Barry: We could take what we learned in our first class—"every exit is an entrance someplace else"—and reframe the comparison, couldn't we? We could say, "Look, Josh Gibson isn't the black Babe Ruth. Instead, Babe Ruth is _______."

Ms. Bristol: The white Josh Gibson.

Prof. Barry: Good. What would we be doing if we did that?

Ms. Bristol: We'd be elevating Josh Gibson above Babe Ruth. We'd be making him the standard.

Prof. Barry: Exactly. It's a nice technique to be aware of, particularly if you're interested in empowering marginalized groups—or even if you're just trying to connect with people.

For example, when John F. Kennedy came to the University of Michigan in October of 1960 to do some campaigning and launch

the idea of the Peace Corps, he did something very similar to what we just did with Josh Gibson. To endear himself to the crowd of folks gathered on the steps of the student union to hear him speak, Kennedy decided not to refer to Michigan as the "Harvard of the Midwest," as many people do. Instead, he referred to Harvard, his alma mater, as?

Ms. Bristol: The Michigan of the East.

Prof. Barry: Why do you think he did that?

Ms. Bristol: To pay Michigan a compliment, to hold it up as the standard by which other universities should be judged.

Prof. Barry: Good. He used the tactic again about a year later in Paris, when he and his increasingly famous wife, Jackie, went on a presidential trip. Beautiful, stylish, and endlessly charming, Jackie received so much attention from the French press that at one point, President Kennedy began a news conference with the following lines.

Ms. Bristol: "I do not think it altogether inappropriate for me to introduce myself to this audience. I am the man who accompanied Jacqueline Kennedy to Paris."

Prof. Barry: Does that remind you of anything from last class?

Ms. Bristol: Yeah. The Amy Poehler line about "Hillary Clinton's husband."

Prof. Barry: Right. We talked about how, during the 2013 Golden Globe Awards, Poehler referred to President Bill Clinton not as President Bill Clinton but as "Hillary Clinton's husband." Kennedy's joke in Paris is a lot like that.

But let's end our review with an example that's a bit closer to home. It is a series of campaign buttons used by another president, University of Michigan alum Gerald Ford, back in the 1970s. During the 1976 election, he tried to capitalize on the popularity of his wife, Betty—

Mr. Carlos (*jumping in***):** Betty Ford?

Prof. Barry: Yeah. Betty Ford.

Mr. Carlos: As in the Betty Ford Center? For addiction?

Prof. Barry: That's her. Even before starting that clinic, she had quite a following—so much so that one of the slogans Gerald Ford's team used to attract voters was "I am betting on Betty's husband."

Mr. Carlos: Really?

Prof. Barry: Yeah. You can see some of the original buttons if you visit the Gerald Ford Museum a couple of hours from here in Grand Rapids, Michigan. It's where Ford grew up and eventually met and married Betty.

It's also where you should all go at some point during ArtPrize, an amazing public art event in which all manner of downtown spaces—banks, bars, hotels, bridges, laundromats—become temporary galleries.

Ms. Cawlow (*jumping in*): I went last year.

Prof. Barry: Did you have fun?

Ms. Cawlow: Yeah. A lot.

Prof. Barry: I figured. ArtPrize is free. It's interactive. And it's full of a whole bunch of creativity, wit, and experimentation.

Which brings us back, in a way, to the person Mr. Dewey asked about at the beginning of class today: James Joyce. Joyce too was full of a whole bunch of creativity, wit, and experimentation. He also wrote an entire book about living as an artist. It's called *A Portrait of the Artist as a Young Man*.

Ms. Cawlow: Does this mean you're finally going to tell that anecdote about him you promised?

Prof. Barry: Yup. I think that now seems like the perfect time.

5

James Joyce

Prof. Barry: Now seems like the perfect time to tell the Joyce anecdote because we've sufficiently reviewed how the words we choose can change the world people see and can now move on to reviewing how the *order* of the words we choose can have a similar effect. Remind everyone, Ms. Nina, what the term for word order is. I believe you helped us with it during our first class.

Ms. Nina: The term for word order is *syntax*, right?

Prof. Barry: Good. As an example, please read what the great tennis player Althea Gibson said separates losers from winners. Her explanation uses a clever bit of syntax.

Ms. Nina: "The loser says it may be possible, but it's difficult; the winner says it may be difficult, but it's possible."

Prof. Barry: Or how about this next statement from Christopher McDougall, the author of a neat book on running called *Born to Run*?

Ms. Nina: "You don't stop running because you get old. You get old because you stop running."

Prof. Barry: Built into each of these constructions is a fancy rhetorical move we'll talk about later in the semester: chiasmus. But for now, I just want us to focus on this notion of syntax, on how the difference between saying "You don't stop running because you get old" and saying "You get old because you stop running" has very little to do with the *choice* of words in the statements and a lot more to do with what, Ms. Nina?

Ms. Nina: The *order* of those words.

Prof. Barry: Exactly. And as we said last time, the order of words—or syntax—is something great writers care deeply about, perhaps none more so than James Joyce. Anybody want to remind us of some of the books he wrote?

Maybe you, Mr. Wild. You mentioned a few in our first class after we learned you are an English major.

Mr. Wild: *Dubliners.*

Prof. Barry: Good. *Dubliners* is the short story collection Joyce published in 1914.

Mr. Wild: *A Portrait of the Artist as a Young Man.*

Prof. Barry: Yup. That's the one I just brought up while talking with Ms. Cawlow. It came out in 1916 and was Joyce's first major novel. And then after that was?

Mr. Wild: *Ulysses.*

Prof. Barry: Very good. That's his masterpiece. It appeared in 1922, on Joyce's fortieth birthday. He loved the fact that while writing it, he reached the approximate age at which Shakespeare wrote *Hamlet* and Dante wrote *Inferno.*

Mr. Wild: There's also *Finnegans Wake.*

Prof. Barry: Right. That was the last book Joyce published, a couple years before his death in 1941. He obsessed over every sentence, as he did with all his books. There are stories of him constantly harassing the printer of *Ulysses,* for example, to see if he would let Joyce make changes to the already displayed text. Estimates are that as much as one-third of that novel was the result of edits Joyce made *after* the printer set the original manuscript pages in type.

Mr. Wild: Is that the anecdote you promised?

Prof. Barry: No. The anecdote I promised appears in a section of the book *On Writing* by Stephen King. Please read that section for us, Mr. Wild.

Mr. Wild: "A friend came to visit [James Joyce] one day and found the great man sprawled across his writing desk in a posture of utter despair."

Prof. Barry: Now read what the friend asked Joyce, and I'll fill in Joyce's responses.

Mr. Wild: "James, what's wrong? Is it the work?"

Prof. Barry: "Yup."

Mr. Wild: "How many words did you get today?"

Prof. Barry: "Seven."

Mr. Wild: "Seven? But James . . . that's *good,* at least for you."

Prof. Barry: "Yes. I suppose it is . . . but I don't know what *order* they go in!"

6

Striking Thirteen

Prof. Barry: I'm not confident that story about Joyce is even true, but it's a great reminder of the importance writers place on finding not just the right word but the right word order. That was part of one of our definitions of good writing from last class. Do you remember it, Mr. Dewey?

Mr. Dewey: Yeah. "Good writing is the best words in their best order."

Prof. Barry: Do you also remember the other two definitions?

Mr. Dewey: "Good writing is getting something right in language."

Prof. Barry: And?

Mr. Dewey: "Good writing is making order out of chaos."

Prof. Barry: Right. We'll want to keep all three of those definitions in mind today as we move on to something we'll call the "Power of the Particular." A great example comes in the opening sentence of George Orwell's classic novel *1984*.

Let's have one of our English majors, Ms. Toth, read it for us.

Ms. Toth: "It was a bright cold day in April, and the clocks were striking thirteen."

Prof. Barry: Compare that to an opening sentence Orwell could have written.

Ms. Toth: "Things were weird."

Prof. Barry: What's better about the original sentence?

Ms. Toth: It's a lot more vivid.

Prof. Barry: And?

Ms. Toth: Specific.

Prof. Barry: How so?

Ms. Toth: Rather than just saying "Things were weird," it gives you a particular image of weirdness to latch on to.

Prof. Barry: What image is that?

Ms. Toth: The clocks striking thirteen.

Prof. Barry: Clocks don't usually do that?

Ms. Toth: No. They usually just go up to twelve.

Prof. Barry: So when you read that a series of clocks are striking thirteen, you think what, exactly?

Ms. Toth: We are in an odd, ominous place.

Prof. Barry: Which is probably?

Ms. Toth: What Orwell wants us to think.

Prof. Barry: Good. By using a concrete image, but using something *particular*, Orwell puts us right inside the dystopian world of Oceania, where *1984* is set. The sentence gives us a really effective

and memorable sense of what that place is like, particularly given that it also alludes to a proverb about how any clock that strikes thirteen calls into question the reliability of the other times it displays as well.

A similarly helpful specificity comes through in the next sentence I want us to look at. It's about the baseball player Jimmie Foxx, a powerful slugger for the Boston Red Sox back in the 1930s and '40s. Read it for us, please, Ms. Toth.

Ms. Toth: "Even his hair had muscles."

Prof. Barry: That description, which is attributed to the Yankees' pitcher Lefty Gomez, is sometimes recorded as "He has muscles in his hair."

Ms. Toth: That doesn't sound as good.

Prof. Barry: I agree. But both are certainly better than a possible alternative: "He was really strong."

Ms. Toth: Right.

Prof. Barry: There's an additional reason, however, that I'm now mentioning Jimmie Foxx: I want us to talk about one of his teammates.

Ms. Toth: Who?

Prof. Barry: Ted Williams.

7

Ted Williams

Prof. Barry: What is so special about Ted Williams, Ms. Bristol?

Ms. Bristol: The way he swung a baseball bat.

Prof. Barry: Which was?

Ms. Bristol: Like nobody before or since.

Prof. Barry: You know some of his more notable accomplishments?

Ms. Bristol: Didn't he win the Triple Crown?

Prof. Barry: He did. Tell everybody what that is.

Ms. Bristol: The Triple Crown is when you lead the league in the three major hitting categories in one season: home runs, RBIs, and batting average.

Prof. Barry: That's kind of hard to do, right? Even doing it once is pretty remarkable.

Ms. Bristol: Yeah.

Prof. Barry: Do you know how many times Williams did it?

Ms. Bristol: Twice?

Prof. Barry: Yup. Once in 1942 and then again in 1947. You know what he did between those years?

Ms. Bristol: What?

Prof. Barry: Fought in World War II.

Ms. Bristol: Right. I forgot about that. He was drafted into the army, wasn't he?

Prof. Barry: Yeah. He never saw any combat in that war, I don't think. But he did become a pilot in the Marine Corps and eventually flew more than thirty missions in Korea during his second stint of service.

Ms. Bristol: He fought in the Korean War too?

Prof. Barry: Yup. At one point, his wingman was a rather famous future astronaut and senator.

Ms. Bristol: Neil Armstrong?

Prof. Barry: No. Armstrong was never a senator.

Ms. Franzoni (*jumping in*)**:** Buzz Aldrin?

Prof. Barry: Nope. It was John Glenn, one of the so-called Mercury Seven, which was the first group of men NASA picked to become American astronauts.

Ms. Bristol: I wonder if Glenn was a Red Sox fan.

Prof. Barry: Probably not. He grew up in Ohio, so he likely rooted for the Cleveland Indians and their star pitcher Bob Feller, who also enlisted during World War II—as did Joe DiMaggio, Warren Spahn, Stan Musial, and Jackie Robinson.

Can you imagine that? All these great players, in the prime of their careers, traded in their gloves and baseball spikes for machine guns and military fatigues. It would be like if when the All-Pro NFL player Pat Tillman signed up for the army following the September 11th attacks, he had also been joined by Brett Favre, Marshall Faulk, and Peyton Manning.

Ms. Bristol: People say Williams's time away from baseball really hurt his career numbers.

Prof. Barry: It's true. He was gone for five years, which makes it even more impressive that he still managed to earn a spot in nineteen All-Star games, including one when he was forty-one years old. He hit .388 that year, becoming the oldest player ever to lead the league in hitting.

But that's not his most famous accomplishment. Nor is, I don't think, what we said earlier—twice winning the Triple Crown. Even that is probably less talked about than something else he managed to do. You know what I'm talking about?

Ms. Bristol: I think so. Williams is the last player to hit .400, right?

Prof. Barry: Exactly. In 1941, the same year that Joe DiMaggio had his famous fifty-six-game hit streak, Ted Williams hit .406, solidifying his place as one of the best—perhaps *the* best—pure hitters of all time.

That was actually his goal: to be the best. In his autobiography, *My Turn at Bat,* he wrote the following, Ms. Bristol.

Ms. Bristol: "A man has to have goals—for a day, for a lifetime—and that was mine, to have people say, 'There goes Ted Williams, the greatest hitter who ever lived.'"

Prof. Barry: What I want to talk about now is an important step Williams took to reach that goal. When he was just starting out with the Red Sox, Williams would make sure to go watch our friend Jimmie Foxx—the guy whose hair had muscles—take batting practice.

Why do you think he did that, Ms. Bristol? Why do you think when Jimmie Foxx warmed up before a game, Williams would stop what he was doing and head over to see Foxx swing?

Ms. Bristol: He probably thought he could learn something.

Prof. Barry: How?

Ms. Bristol: Because Jimmie Foxx was a really good player, and you can learn a lot just by watching someone like that in action.

Prof. Barry: Good. Here's a principle that captures that thought.

Ms. Bristol: "To play good baseball, you need to watch good baseball."

Prof. Barry: Now let's add a related principle, this time from the world of music. We get it from a story about the great jazz saxophonist Charlie Parker once taking a job as a dishwasher at

Jimmie's Chicken Shack in New York—not because he liked scraping fried chicken and mashed potatoes off of dirty plates but because he wanted to hear another great jazz artist, Art Tatum, play the piano there each night.

Where's Ms. Nina, our musician?

Ms. Nina: Here.

Prof. Barry: Can you read the music principle for us, please?

Ms. Nina: "To play good music, you need to listen to good music."

Prof. Barry: Do you think that's true, at least in your experience?

Ms. Nina: Definitely. Everyone in my program has particular people they want to sound like.

Prof. Barry: So you're pretty deliberate about what you listen to?

Ms. Nina: Most of the time, yeah.

Prof. Barry: Would you be surprised to learn that really good painters might be the same way—although with things they look at, not necessarily things they listen to? We could point to the Impressionist painter Édouard Manet, for example, and note his decision, early on in his career, to spend hour after hour at the Louvre in Paris studying the great works on display. Which means, for him, the principle might be?

Ms. Nina: "To paint good paintings, you need to look at good paintings."

Prof. Barry: Exactly. So now let's try to connect all this to writing. "To write good sentences," we might say?

Ms. Nina: "You need to read good sentences."

Prof. Barry: Perfect. I tell this to my law students all the time, citing similar statements by two of the best legal writers of the past century: Chief Justice John Roberts and Judge Frank Easterbrook.

Here, for example, is what Chief Justice Roberts told writing expert Bryan Garner back in 2007. Want to read it for us, Mr. Marshall? Given your plans to head off to law school, you might want to pay particular attention to it.

Mr. Marshall: "The only good way to learn about writing is to read good writing."

Prof. Barry: And here is Judge Easterbrook, one of the most revered federal appellate judges in the country, on the same subject. I actually got to take two of his classes during my time in law school at the University of Chicago.

Mr. Marshall: "The best way to become a better legal writer is to spend more time reading good prose."

Prof. Barry: Easterbrook specifically recommends the novels of Ernest Hemingway, William Faulkner, and Saul Bellow, although he also says much can be learned from regularly reading well-edited magazines like the *Atlantic* and *Commentary*.

Keep in mind, however, that when we read any good writing, we'll want to pay attention not just to its content but also to its composition—how it was put together word by word and sentence by sentence. We'll want to learn, to a certain extent, how to start "reading like a writer," which is the title of a neat book by Francine Prose, the author of several novels, short stories, and works of nonfiction. This is how she describes her approach.

Mr. Marshall: "Too often students are being taught to read as if literature were some kind of ethics class or civics class—or worse, some kind of self-help manual. In fact, the important thing is the way the writer uses the language."

Prof. Barry: She then goes on to say the following.

Mr. Marshall: "Every so often I'll hear writers say that there are other writers they would read if for no other reason than to marvel at the skill with which they can put together the sort of sentences that move us to read closely, to disassemble and reassemble them, much the way a mechanic might learn about an engine by taking it apart."

Prof. Barry: In this course, we are going to try to become those mechanic-like writers. We'll study how sentences are constructed and how their various parts work together to communicate information clearly, effectively, and sometimes beautifully. We'll start with a sentence from a somewhat surprising place, at least for literary craftsmanship.

Mr. Marshall: Where?

Prof. Barry: A car ad.

8

Electric Clock

Prof. Barry: Would you please read the sentence for us, Ms. Bart? You've become our go-to person for all things marketing and business.

Ms. Bart: Sure.

Prof. Barry: Great. It comes from an ad for Rolls-Royce back in 1959.

Ms. Bart: "At 60 miles an hour the loudest noise in this new Rolls-Royce comes from the electric clock."

Prof. Barry: Compare that to this sentence.

Ms. Bart: "This new Rolls-Royce is really quiet."

Prof. Barry: What's better about the first sentence, the one that mentions the electric clock?

Ms. Bart: It does what we said the Orwell sentence does and what the "hair had muscles" sentence does.

Prof. Barry: Which is?

Ms. Bart: It creates an image.

Prof. Barry: What kind of image?

Ms. Bart: The kind of image that gives you a sense of just how quiet that car must be.

Prof. Barry: Right. And it does that by using something *particular*. It doesn't talk in generalities. It doesn't use vague, unhelpful language. Instead, it fastens onto something compellingly concrete: the sound of the electric clock.

Let's try to do that with our own writing. Let's move past abstractions. Let's avoid fuzzy phrasing. Let's harness the Power of the Particular. As William Strunk Jr. and E. B. White point out in *The Elements of Style*, "If those who have studied the art of writing are in accord on any one point, it is this: the surest way to arouse and hold the reader's attention is by being specific, definite, and concrete." Would you mind finishing that quote for us, Ms. Bart?

Ms. Bart: "The greatest writers—Homer, Dante, Shakespeare—are effective largely because they deal in particulars and report the details that matter. Their words call up pictures."

Prof. Barry: Poet Mary Oliver gets at the same idea when she writes the following sentence in a book called *A Poetry Handbook*.

Ms. Bart: "The language of the poem is the language of particulars."

Prof. Barry: And so does Mary Karr in her book *The Art of Memoir*, which we'll return to later in today's class.

Ms. Bart: "In some magic way, the detail from its singular position in a room can help to evoke the rest of the whole scene."

Prof. Barry: But to give you a closer look at the Power of the Particular in action, we're going to move out of the world of literature and into the world of politics. Which means it's time to return to President Kennedy.

9

Before This Decade Is Out

Prof. Barry: We said earlier, Ms. Burke, that Kennedy helped launch the Peace Corps when he spoke to that crowd of students at the Michigan Union in October 1960.

Ms. Burke: Right.

Prof. Barry: Well, he also helped launch an even bigger endeavor when he spoke to Congress about eight months later as president. Do you know what I'm talking about?

Ms. Burke: I think so. Does it involve the astronaut we mentioned before?

Prof. Barry: John Glenn?

Ms. Burke: Yeah.

Prof. Barry: It does.

Ms. Burke: And the other two—Neil Armstrong and Buzz Aldrin?

Prof. Barry: Yup. But Glenn actually retired from NASA before Armstrong and Aldrin took their first space flights.

Ms. Burke: Those three never flew together?

Prof. Barry: No, they didn't. Glenn, as I mentioned earlier, was the first American to orbit the earth. Armstrong and Aldrin were the first to walk on the moon.

Ms. Burke: Got it.

Prof. Barry: All, however, were part of the major initiative Kennedy introduced: putting a man on the moon.

Addressing a special joint session of Congress on May 25, 1961, Kennedy said the following, Ms. Burke.

Ms. Burke: "I believe that this nation should commit itself to achieving the goal, before this decade is out, of landing a man on the moon and returning him safely to the earth."

Prof. Barry: See how particular that is, how specific? Kennedy doesn't say, "I believe that this nation should commit itself to achieving the goal sometime in the future." He doesn't offer some

open-ended timeline for which nobody can really be held accountable. He says, “Before this decade is out.”

Ms. Burke: Right.

Prof. Barry: Nor does he say we should simply commit ourselves to “increasing space exploration.” That would be too vague and not very inspiring. Instead, Kennedy uses a goal that is as concrete as it is ambitious: putting a man on the moon.

Ms. Burke: And returning him safely to the earth.

Prof. Barry: Right. That’s an important part of any space flight. You have to be able to bring the astronauts back.

Which NASA did, thankfully. Armstrong and Aldrin landed on the moon on July 20, 1969, and they—along with a third astronaut, Michael Collins—splashed down safely in the Pacific Ocean four days later.

Ms. Burke: So NASA hit the deadline Kennedy identified.

Prof. Barry: Yeah. Kennedy gave his speech in May 1961. And by the end of July 1969, the astronauts had landed on the moon and made it all the way back home.

Ms. Burke: Before the decade was out.

Prof. Barry: Right. Before the decade was out.

10

No Ideas but in Things

Prof. Barry: Our next example, also from the world of politics, has a similarly happy ending. Have you ever heard of President Ronald Reagan, Ms. Burke? Has his name come up in any of your political science classes?

Ms. Burke: Yeah, a few times.

Prof. Barry: Good. Well, one of his most famous moments as president came on June 12, 1987, when he gave a speech in front of the Brandenburg Gate in Germany, a site very near the Berlin Wall. This was at the end of the Cold War, so West Germany and East Germany were still essentially two separate countries. In fact, they had two separate World Cup soccer teams. West Germany won the World Cup in 1990, but that same year, East Germany didn't even qualify.

Ms. Burke: It's so weird to think there were once two Germanys.

Prof. Barry: I know. But think how you'd feel if you grew up before they unified. To those folks, it was probably weird to think there would ever be just *one* Germany.

Imagine telling members of the 1976 West German swim team, for example, that they would eventually share a flag with all their East German counterparts, the ones who engaged in the most systematic abuse of steroids in Olympic history. That must have taken some getting used to. Or imagine saying to them, "Look, from now on, you'll all sing the same national anthem."

Ms. Burke: Yeah. I doubt that went over well.

Prof. Barry: The part of Reagan's speech we're going to look at, however, was not aimed at either of the Germanys. It was aimed at the Soviet Union. Reagan had spent much of his two terms as president trying to hasten the fall of communism, even going so far as to call the Soviet Union the "Evil Empire."

That motivation helps explain why he took full advantage of his symbolic position in front of the Brandenburg Gate during the speech—the divisive Berlin Wall looming all around him—to address the leader of that empire directly. Any chance you know the name of that leader?

Ms. Burke: Gorbachev?

Prof. Barry: Yup. Mikhail Gorbachev. But before we look at what Reagan actually said to Gorbachev, let's look at what he could have said. Doing that will highlight an added benefit of the Power of the Particular: it often helpfully eliminates a lot of words.

Ms. Burke: So what I am about to read is what Reagan *could* have said?

Prof. Barry: Yeah. If he had really bad speech writers.

Ms. Burke: "Mr. Gorbachev, please begin the elimination of the elaborate and inefficient system of totalitarian government that is

currently resulting in the censorship of the press, the stagnation of your economy, and the oppression of millions of people."

Prof. Barry: Fortunately, however, Reagan had really good speech writers. So the world was treated to the following memorable line.

Ms. Burke: "Mr. Gorbachev, tear down this wall!"

Prof. Barry: See how much better that is? With one concrete detail, one powerful image, you can replace a whole paragraph of bureaucratic bombast. You can give your audience something they can grasp, remember, and maybe even repeat.

Ms. Burke: Right.

Prof. Barry: It's sort of like an observation Thomas Friedman includes in his best-selling book *The World Is Flat*. He's quoting Stanley Fischer, an accomplished economist who has held prominent positions at the International Monetary Fund, the Bank of Israel, and the United States Federal Reserve. Read it for us, please, Ms. Burke.

Ms. Burke: "One good example is worth one thousand theories."

Prof. Barry: Few people can keep one thousand theories in their heads at once. Few people are going to be persuaded by that level of abstraction. But a good example—now that can really move people.

More support for this approach comes from the neurologist Oliver Sacks, who often focused on telling the stories of individual patients in his books, including *The Man Who Mistook His Wife for a Hat* and the book that inspired an Oscar-nominated movie starring Robin Williams and Robert De Niro, *Awakenings*. Here's how he once described the benefits of his strategy. He's recalling a conversation he had with the chief doctor at the Einstein College of Medicine in the Bronx, which is where Sacks worked for many years. They are talking about "L-dopa," the drug in *Awakenings* that helps patients break out of their catatonic state. Let's have Mr. Carlos read it for us.

Mr. Carlos: "'How many patients do you have on L-dopa?' [the chief doctor] asked."

Prof. Barry: Now read Sacks's answer.

Mr. Carlos: "'Three sir,' I replied eagerly."

Prof. Barry: To which the chief said?

Mr. Carlos: "Gee, Oliver. I have three *hundred* patients on L-dopa."

Prof. Barry: A little hurt by the chief's tone, Sacks then offers the following retort.

Mr. Carlos: "Yes, but I learn a hundred times as much about each patient as you do."

Prof. Barry: At a different point in the book, Sacks even suggests that while clinical trials of large groups of people are certainly important, "one needs the concrete, the particular, the personal too." He then suggests the following.

Mr. Carlos: "It is impossible to convey the nature and impact of any neurological condition *without* entering and describing the lives of individual patients."

Prof. Barry: Don't get me wrong, though. Sacks doesn't advocate abandoning scientific investigation that is more large scale, abstract, or both. And neither do I. There is tremendous value in that kind of research.

My point is simply that even in a world that covets large sample sizes and scatter plots, there's still a place for the particular, for that telling detail or individual story that brings with it a great deal of insight and illumination. "No ideas but in things," the modernist poet William Carlos Williams famously wrote over and over again in his five-volume epic poem *Patterson*—and it's not as if he had an unscientific mind. When he wasn't writing poetry, he was what you want to be, Mr. Carlos.

Mr. Carlos: He was a doctor?

Prof. Barry: Yeah. For more than forty years, Williams saw all manner of patients in his home state of New Jersey. He'd deliver a baby in the morning and then work on his poetry at night. Sort of like Anton Chekhov, the Russian playwright and short story writer.

Mr. Carlos: Chekhov was a doctor too?

Prof. Barry: Yeah. He claimed medicine was his wife and literature was his mistress.

"Whenever I get tired of one," he explained, "I spend the night with the other."

More importantly for our purposes, however, Chekhov, like Williams, really championed what we've been calling the Power of the Particular. We're about to see evidence of that in a letter he wrote to his brother Alexander back in 1886. Chekhov tries to give him some writing advice.

11

Any Idiot Can Face a Crisis

Prof. Barry: Would you please read the advice from Chekhov for us, Ms. Yona? I'm guessing you've come across some of his work on a syllabus or two in your comparative literature classes.

Ms. Yona: Yeah. I've been assigned his stuff a few times.

Prof. Barry: Mostly his plays?

Ms. Yona: No. Mostly his short stories.

Prof. Barry: Those are good too. Remember Francine Prose, the author of that book *Reading Like a Writer* we talked about earlier in the class?

Ms. Yona: Yeah.

Prof. Barry: She's a huge fan of Chekhov's short stories. There's a whole section in that book called "Learning from Chekhov."

Ms. Yona: Is that where you found the letter to his brother?

Prof. Barry: No. I found it on a great website called Quote Investigator. Created by someone with a PhD from Yale who goes by the pseudonym Garson O'Toole, the site is the best source I know for clearing up misattributed quotations. It has a great entry, for example, on a quip for which Chekhov often gets undeserved credit: "Any idiot can survive a crisis; it's this day-to-day living that wears you out."

Ms. Yona: Chekhov didn't write that?

Prof. Barry: Apparently not.

Ms. Yona: Then who did?

Prof. Barry: A screenwriter named George Seaton. In the 1954 movie *The Country Girl*—which features big-name actors Bing Crosby, Grace Kelly, and William Holden—Seaton has Crosby's character say at one point, "Just about anybody can face a crisis. It's that everyday living that's rough."

Ms. Yona: So then why do so many people attribute the quote to Chekhov? I think I've seen it on Instagram a bunch of times. And it's always attached to Chekhov, never to the Seaton guy.

Prof. Barry: Well, which do you think sounds more impressive: quoting Chekhov or quoting a somewhat obscure screenwriter?

Plus, "Any idiot can survive a crisis" kind of sounds like something Chekhov might write. He was the great chronicler of the ordinary, the mundane, the miniature—which is partly why he's such a great person through which to learn the Power of the Particular. He wasn't Tolstoy or Dostoevsky. He didn't have grand theories or plots. But he did pay careful attention to small details.

All this comes through in the advice he gives his brother in that letter I mentioned. Here it is.

Ms. Yona: "In descriptions of Nature, one must seize on small details, grouping them so that when the reader closes his eyes he gets a picture."

Prof. Barry: He then offers an example.

Ms. Yona: "For instance, you'll have a moonlit night if you write that on the mill dam a piece of glass from a broken bottle glittered like a bright little star, and that the black shadow of a dog or a wolf rolled past like a ball."

Prof. Barry: Through translations and other modifications, that advice has morphed over the years into the following directive.

Ms. Yona: "Don't tell me the moon is shining; show me the glint of light on broken glass."

Prof. Barry: Which is very similar to perhaps the most common writing advice of all time. Read it for us.

Ms. Yona: "Show, don't tell."

Prof. Barry: Exactly. "Show, don't tell." You hear that in school. You hear that out of school. You hear that everywhere people are learning to write. But as we are about to learn, there is a way that, at least in certain circumstances, it might actually be bad advice.

12

Show and Tell

Prof. Barry: When I say that "Show, don't tell" might be bad advice, I don't mean that what Chekhov told his brother was wrong. Insisting that good writers "seize on small details" is extremely helpful, as is explaining that it's important to group those details together "so that when the reader closes his eyes he gets a picture."

That's exactly what we've been talking about today, isn't it, Ms. Yona?

Ms. Yona: Yeah.

Prof. Barry: The tricky part is figuring out when to do that kind of showing and when to take a different approach. You can't *just* show and never tell. You'll overwhelm your reader. Excessive details are ruinous.

Ms. Yona: So are we supposed to *not* show?

Prof. Barry: No. You're supposed to show. But you also need, in many situations, to *tell*. We can return to Francine Prose, the superfan of Chekhov, for a fuller explanation of this point. Please read her description of a great passage from Alice Munro, who won the 2013 Nobel Prize in literature and is an expert when it comes to knowing the proper mix of showing and telling.

Ms. Yona: "The passage contradicts a form of bad advice often given young writers—namely, that the job of the author is to show, not tell."

Prof. Barry: Keep reading.

Ms. Yona: "Needless to say, many great novelists combine 'dramatic' showing with long sections of the flat-out authorial narration that is, I guess, what is meant by telling."

Prof. Barry: See? Show *and* tell. Great writers, Prose says, do both. She then talks about the danger that comes with thinking you should only show.

Ms. Yona: "[It] leads to a confusion that causes novice writers to think that everything should be acted out . . . when in fact the responsibility of showing should be assumed by the energetic and specific use of language."

Prof. Barry: For additional support, let's turn to another master of composition, Phillip Lopate. He gives a similar endorsement of the show-and-tell approach in a book about the craft of literary nonfiction. It is called, appropriately enough, *To Show and To Tell.*

Ms. Yona: "It seems obviously desirable for a writing style to be able to move freely and easily from the concrete to the general and back."

Prof. Barry: I've underlined that last phrase because I think it is so important. From "the concrete to the general and back" is exactly the kind of writing we'll be shooting for in this course. We'll want to produce writing that isn't full of abstractions but also isn't afraid of them. We'll want our words to be earthy and alive, vivid and affecting—yet at the same time analytic and expository.

Which means we're going to have to work hard to apply two concepts that perhaps Ms. Toth has learned about in one of her creative writing classes.

Ms. Toth: I think I might know which ones you're talking about.

Prof. Barry: The first is summary.

Ms. Toth: Yup.

Prof. Barry: And the second one is?

Ms. Toth: Scene.

Prof. Barry: Good. Summary and scene. We'll tackle those next.

13

Summary and Scene

Prof. Barry: Tell us a little about the distinction between summary and scene, Ms. Toth. How is a summary different from a scene?

Ms. Toth: A summary is more general and usually covers a longer span of time.

Prof. Barry: So with a summary, writers typically describe more than just a single event or development, right?

Ms. Toth: Right. They describe many events and developments.

Prof. Barry: Good. And they also provide other things along with those descriptions. What are some of them?

Ms. Toth: Maybe a little analysis.

Prof. Barry: Yup. What else?

Ms. Toth: Context?

Prof. Barry: Good. Summary, at least as we'll be using the term, often involves context. It's a way of communicating a lot of information in a short amount of space. There's synthesis. There's compression. There's value added by collecting and condensing a wide range of material.

A great example in fiction comes in the novel *To the Lighthouse* by Virginia Woolf. The book is filled with many exquisite scenes—by which I mean individual settings and moments relayed in close, beautiful detail. But one of the most remarkable sections is a powerful bit of summary.

Ms. Toth: "Time Passes"?

Prof. Barry: Yeah. The section is called "Time Passes." Have you read *To the Lighthouse*?

Ms. Toth: I'm reading it now in a class on literary modernism. We just got to that section.

Prof. Barry: Is the class with John Whittier-Ferguson?

Ms. Toth: Yes.

Prof. Barry: Isn't he the best?

Ms. Toth: He is. He's awesome.

Prof. Barry: I was a TA for one of his classes back when I was in graduate school. It was where I first read *To the Lighthouse*. At the time, I was probably still too clueless to pick up on just how magical that "Time Passes" section is. It's really a fabulous bit of writing. In just twenty pages, Woolf covers ten years in the lives of her characters. People marry. People die. A house deteriorates and then is brought back to life.

And . . . there's a war.

Ms. Toth: We talked about that in my class. It's World War I, right?

Prof. Barry: Right. The events in the "Time Passes" section start in 1910 and end in 1920. World War I falls right in the middle of that.

But we don't have to travel all the way back to the beginning of the twentieth century to find helpful examples of summary and scene. Nor do we have to read classic works of literature. We can do something much more commonplace and contemporary, something that many of you probably do every day—maybe even two or three times a day.

Ms. Toth: What?

Prof. Barry: Watch *SportsCenter*.

14

This Is *SportsCenter*

Prof. Barry: Ms. Bristol, what is *SportsCenter*?

Ms. Bristol: It's a news program.

Prof. Barry: About?

Ms. Bristol: Sports.

Prof. Barry: What network is it on?

Ms. Bristol: ESPN.

Prof. Barry: Has it always been on ESPN?

Ms. Bristol: You mean, was it ever on another network?

Prof. Barry: No. I mean, was there ever an ESPN without *SportsCenter*? Was there ever a time when the network existed but *SportsCenter* hadn't yet been created?

Ms. Bristol: I don't think so. Wasn't an episode of *SportsCenter* the first show to air on ESPN?

Prof. Barry: Yeah. It was how ESPN announced itself to the world.

Ms. Bristol: That's what I thought.

Prof. Barry: Do you know when that was? Do you know when ESPN launched?

Ms. Bristol: The 1980s?

Prof. Barry: Close.

Ms. Bristol: The 1970s?

Prof. Barry: Yup. On September 7, 1979—the same year that Margaret Thatcher was elected prime minister of the UK and Michael Jackson released his first solo album—American viewers got their first glimpse of what has become one of the most popular and powerful networks on television. The opening lines on the inaugural show were uttered by Lee Leonard, one of the two original *SportsCenter* anchors. He said something like this: "If you're a sports fan, what you will see in the next minutes, hours, and days to follow may convince you that you've gone to heaven."

Ms. Bristol: And the rest is history?

Prof. Barry: Kind of. In 1995, *SportsCenter* apparently passed *CBS News* as the most-televised live show of all time. No doubt that's because *SportsCenter* is on multiple times a day. Few live shows have that advantage. Still, the success of the show is phenomenal.

Ms. Bristol: I watch it at least twice a day, sometimes three or four times.

Mr. Boh (*jumping in*)**:** I'd live in *SportsCenter* if I could.

Prof. Barry: Millions of other viewers would probably join you, Mr. Boh. Yet it's important to remember that there was nothing inevitable about *SportsCenter* becoming a hit. Nor about ESPN even being created. A lot of people were skeptical of the idea of a network completely devoted to sports, as the book *Those Guys Have All the Fun: Inside the World of ESPN* makes clear. One of my favorite moments from that book is when the eventual CEO of ESPN,

Stuart Evey, recounts a conversation he had with the then head of HBO, a person who thought ESPN would never find an audience. Read Evey's version of that conversation for us, please, Mr. Boh.

Mr. Boh: "I talked to [the HBO guy] about what he thought of this idea we were considering and he said, 'There's no way anybody will ever watch sports twenty-four hours a day.'"

Prof. Barry: Isn't that great? I love those kinds of predictions. Not because I think the person who made it probably didn't have good reasons for thinking what he did. You don't get to be the head of HBO by making baseless bets on what will and won't be successful.

I love it because it's a good reminder of a much-repeated observation: "Predictions are hard, especially about the future."

15

Being a Bore

Prof. Barry: The reason I say *SportsCenter* is a good place to learn about summary and scene is that the people who run the show are especially skilled at moving back and forth between those two modes of communication. They know how to pair detailed looks at specific moments in a game with more broadscale, context-providing sections of narration. Don't you think so, Mr. Boh?

Mr. Boh: Definitely.

Prof. Barry: Take highlights, for example. Highlights are the prototypical summary and scene situation. You can't show the entire game when doing highlights. You can't include every little thing that happened. You have to summarize a bit. You have to not just show but also tell.

At the same time, however, you can't *only* tell. You can't only use summary. You need to include at least a few scenes every now and then. Why do you think that is, Mr. Boh? Why do you think you need a good mix of both summary and scene when doing highlights? What does that combination give viewers?

Mr. Boh: It gives them a chance to experience the key moments in a game.

Prof. Barry: Without?

Mr. Boh: Having to sit through the un-key moments.

Prof. Barry: So in football, highlights might include?

Mr. Boh: The touchdowns.

Prof. Barry: And leave out?

Mr. Boh: The huddles.

Prof. Barry: And with baseball, highlights might include?

Mr. Boh: The home runs.

Prof. Barry: And leave out?

Mr. Boh: The foul balls.

Prof. Barry: How about with tennis? What do you think highlights might include there?

Mr. Boh: Maybe the breaks of serve and set points?

Prof. Barry: And what might they leave out?

Mr. Boh: The changeovers.

Prof. Barry: You mean where the players grab some water and switch sides?

Mr. Boh: Yeah. Those rarely warrant a scene.

Prof. Barry: I agree—except, of course, for the changeover that happened back in 1993, when Monica Seles, the number-one player in the world at the time, was attacked by a spectator. Do you know anything about that, Mr. Boh?

Mr. Boh: Yeah. Didn't the guy run out of the stands and stab her?

Prof. Barry: He did. In Seles's back. With a boning knife.

Ms. Henrietta (*jumping in***):** Gross.

Prof. Barry: You think that changeover made the highlights, Mr. Boh?

Mr. Boh: Definitely.

Prof. Barry: So it could be the case that with the other examples we mentioned—huddles in football, foul balls in baseball—the things that we suggested were un-key and likely to be left out might actually turn out to be *very* key and likely to be left in, at least in certain circumstances. Think, for example, of the record-breaking sixteen foul balls Brandon Belt of the San Francisco Giants hit during one marathon at bat against the Los Angeles Angels in 2018. You think some of those made *SportsCenter*?

Mr. Boh: I would think so, yeah.

Prof. Barry: Most fouls balls are unremarkable. But sixteen in one at-bat seems like something people might want to see. Which means that what typically might be tucked into a summary or possibly skipped over completely can sometimes transform into its own gripping scene.

Mr. Boh: Right.

Prof. Barry: Yet my point is somewhat broader than that. To put together a good set of highlights, you have to develop many of the same qualities we want to develop as writers. You have to be selective. You have to demonstrate restraint. You have to balance showing with telling.

The proper ratio is not a scientific formula, but the more you consider the way each complements the other—the more you balance summaries with scenes, synthesis with specifics—the better your writing will be. Same goes, perhaps, for your job prospects at ESPN.

16

Sentences Nobody Else Could Write

Prof. Barry: We just said that balancing synthesis with specifics is important. But given that the focus of today's class is specifics, we're going to spend much less time on synthesis and much more time on specifics. The plan is to become alert to "the unnoticed things that [make] emotions," which is what Ernest Hemingway told the *Paris Review* he searched for when he first started out as a writer back in the 1920s in Chicago. Here are the examples he gave the interviewer. Please read the first one for us, Ms. Maat.

Ms. Maat: "The way an outfielder tossed his glove without looking back where it fell."

Prof. Barry: Now the second.

Ms. Maat: "The squeak of resin on canvas under a fighter's flat-soled gym shoes."

Prof. Barry: And finally, the third. As we'll learn next class, people—including Hemingway—tend to group information in sets of three.

Ms. Maat: "The gray color of Jack Blackburn's skin when he had just come out of a stir."

Prof. Barry: You see how specific each of those descriptions are? Take that last one: "The gray color of Jack Blackburn's skin when he had just come out of a stir."

Ms. Ida (*jumping in*): Who's Jack Blackburn?

Prof. Barry: He was a boxer, a really good boxer. He also eventually became the trainer of Joe Louis, the longtime heavyweight champion and a native son of Detroit. Hemingway, a huge fan of boxing, must have seen Blackburn fight when Blackburn was still a title contender.

Ms. Ida: Got it.

Prof. Barry: Knowing who he is helps us appreciate the level of detail Hemingway uses in his descriptions. Hemingway doesn't just say "the gray color" of any boxer's skin, right, Ms. Ida? He says "the gray color of Jack Blackburn's skin." He picks a particular boxer.

Ms. Ida: Right.

Prof. Barry: He also doesn't just say "the gray color of Jack Blackburn's skin" in general. He says "the gray color of Jack Blackburn's skin" at a unique instance: "when he is coming out of a stir." That narrowing, that precision, can really help create an effective image.

Ms. Ida: Like with the second sentence: "The squeak of resin on canvas under a fighter's flat-soled gym shoes."

Prof. Barry: Exactly. See how each detail makes the sentence more and more evocative? See how it just wouldn't be the same if Hemingway had stopped at "The squeak of resin on canvas"? Or if he had simply said, "The squeak of resin under gym shoes"?

Ms. Ida: Yeah. Those sentences are much more bland and forgettable.

Prof. Barry: Or take a sentence attributed to Joyce Carol Oates, a writer who shares Hemingway's fascination with boxing. She wrote a whole book on the subject. It's called *On Boxing*, and it's really good—although in this example, she's talking about writing.

Ms. Ida: "Getting the first draft finished is like pushing a peanut with your nose across a very dirty floor."

Prof. Barry: Isn't that awesome? I love that she uses something as specific as a peanut and that she makes the floor not just any floor but "a very dirty floor."

Ms. Ida: The bit about pushing with your nose is a nice touch as well.

Prof. Barry: Yeah. It's a fantastic touch, the kind of thing that can really distinguish you as a writer as well as a skillful communicator more generally. Think of really good stand-up comedians like Richard Pryor, Chris Rock, Ellen DeGeneres, George Carlin, and Ali Wong. All of them built their careers by expressing themselves with hilarious specificity. They focused exactly on what Hemingway said: the unnoticed things that make emotions.

Ms. Ida: Right.

Prof. Barry: Eddie Murphy is another comedian who does this incredibly well. Go watch his performances in comedy specials like

Delirious or *Raw*. Listen for the details he uses when telling his stories or when doing his impressions. They're what make his jokes.

Mr. Farnoff (*jumping in*)**:** How about Jerry Seinfeld?

Prof. Barry: Jerry Seinfeld is a great example. Same with his fellow creator of *Seinfeld*, Larry David. Their approach to observational humor, their ability to make comedic gold out of the minutia of everyday life, aligns well with a piece of advice Hemingway supposedly gave writer Archibald MacLeish. "Experience," Hemingway is supposed to have said, "is communicated by small details, intimately preserved."

Mr. Farnoff: That's pretty good.

Prof. Barry: There is a way to see the entire concept of *Seinfeld*—as well Larry David's show, *Curb Your Enthusiasm*—through the lens of that advice.

Actually, there's a way to see a lot of shows through the lens of that advice—and a lot of movies, songs, paintings, and poems too. Creative expression seems to go well when it strikes audiences as thoughtfully original, when it contains aspects of lived experience that are so particular that they feel personal.

Which is why I often give the following advice to students working on personal essays, especially ones they may end up borrowing from to write application essays and cover letters. Read the advice for us, please, Mr. Farnoff.

Mr. Farnoff: "Try to write sentences nobody else could write."

17

Sincerity Sometimes Takes a Few Drafts

Prof. Barry: Ms. Toth, what do you think I mean by the phrase Mr. Farnoff just read for us: "Try to write sentences nobody else could write"?

Ms. Toth: That you should avoid clichés.

Prof. Barry: What else?

Ms. Toth: That you should try to focus on something unique to you.

Prof. Barry: Good. Suppose you grew up in Russia, as one of my law students did. Suppose as well that the way you taught yourself English, when you came over to the United States in your early twenties, was by watching hours and hours of the sitcom *How I Met Your Mother*. Is that something you might want to include in an application essay? Is that the kind of thing nobody else could write?

Ms. Toth: Definitely.

Prof. Barry: What about if he had just written, "I taught myself English by watching television"?

Ms. Toth: That's not as good.

Prof. Barry: "I taught myself English"?

Ms. Toth: Even worse.

Prof. Barry: How come?

Ms. Toth: Because a lot of people have taught themselves English. It doesn't make the student stand out as much.

Prof. Barry: But identifying the actual show—that helps?

Ms. Toth: Yeah. I think so, especially because the show turned out to be *How I Met Your Mother*. It's not like he said *Masterpiece Theater* or something.

Prof. Barry: Right. *Masterpiece Theater* might seem a little contrived and snooty.

Ms. Toth: Yeah. Like the student was trying too hard to sound smart. Like he made it up.

Prof. Barry: But *How I Met Your Mother*?

Ms. Toth: That sounds like it might actually be true. It sounds sincere.

Prof. Barry: It was sincere. The student did teach himself English by watching hours and hours of the sitcom *How I Met Your Mother*. But here's the thing: I only found that out by reading the first draft of his essay with him, where he wrote a much more generic sentence that essentially said, "I taught myself English by watching a lot of television."

Ms. Toth: So you got him to change it?

Prof. Barry: Yeah. I told him that what he wrote was too general, that he was missing out on the opportunity to create a memorable image—something that might stick with his audience, in a very positive way.

And I simply asked him, "What was the television show you watched the most?" When he said, laughing a little bit, *How I Met Your Mother*, I said, "Okay. Now rewrite the sentence."

Ms. Toth: And he did? With *How I Met Your Mother* in it?

Prof. Barry: Yeah. It took three or four tries to get the wording right. But the sentence he eventually wrote did a much better job of capturing his personality and background.

There's a lesson there. We often think that being sincere means being unfiltered, that the first thought that pops in our head is the best representation of our true self. But what my student discovered is that patience, revision, and flexibility have roles to play as well. So here's a bit of advice. It applies to applications, essays, and cover letters, and it also applies to personal letters, recommendation letters, and other heartfelt correspondences. Read it for us, please, Ms. Toth.

Ms. Toth: "Sometimes sincerity takes a few drafts."

18

Strive for Five

Prof. Barry: When I say that sincerity takes a few drafts, I'm not joking. It takes practice to sound authentic, at least when it comes to writing. Our initial attempts are often full of boringly bland statements. Michael Eric Dyson, who teaches in the sociology department at Georgetown and often provides commentary for ESPN, has a way of describing the tremendous work it can take to craft words and ideas that sound natural. Read the following passage for us, please, Ms. Burke. It comes from Dyson's award-winning book *What Truth Sounds Like*.

Ms. Burke: "Writing beckons one to revisit over an extended, or at least delayed, period the same material and to revise what one thinks."

Prof. Barry: Keep going.

Ms. Burke: "Revision is reading again and again what one writes so that one can think again and again about what one wants to say and in turn determine if better and deeper things can be said."

Prof. Barry: None of that is easy. But who promised you easy? I certainly never make that guarantee on the syllabus. There's no section in it that begins with "Welcome to the Syntax of Sports. Prepare to coast."

Instead, I try to make clear that this course is designed to challenge you. You're going to think new things, try new things, and write new things. That isn't always an enjoyable process. But according to my former students, it does pay off—and not just in the writing you do here at Michigan. It also pays off in places like med school, law school, business school, Wall Street, and Silicon Valley. Even if we just focus on all the communicating you do via email, becoming good with words is a real professional asset.

So with that in mind, I want you all to learn to do something that might be a little hard at first, especially given the attention we've paid today to using the Power of the Particular to create memorable images: I want you to move beyond the visual realm.

Ms. Cawlow (*jumping in*): In our minds?

Prof. Barry: No. On the page. We sometimes forget that the sense of sight is just one of the senses our writing can evoke. There are four other ones that can be just as, if not more, effective. Can you please name them for us, Ms. Cawlow?

Ms. Cawlow: Sure. The sense of smell. The sense of touch. The sense of taste. And the sense of hearing.

Prof. Barry: Right. Wouldn't it be great if a piece of writing engaged all of those senses—in addition to engaging the sense of sight?

Ms. Maat (*jumping in*): You want our writing to smell?

Prof. Barry: Not literally, no. But I do want your writing to describe how things smell, just as I want it to describe how things sound and taste and feel. Only focusing on one sense isn't enough, especially if it's the sense of sight over and over again. I want you to "strive for five."

Ms. Maat: You want us to hit all five senses?

Prof. Barry: Not in every sentence. Not in every paragraph. Maybe not even in every assignment you turn in. But I at least want the following idea on your creative radar: the Power of the Particular is not limited to sight alone.

Take Supreme Court Justice Sonia Sotomayor, for example. We talked about her during our first class. I think it was you, Ms. Yona, who mentioned her memoir, *My Beloved World*.

Ms. Yona: Yeah. My mom gives it to practically everyone she meets.

Prof. Barry: Good. In it, Sotomayor shares what she did to connect with jurors back when she was a prosecutor in New York, which was her first job after graduating from Yale Law School in 1979. Read a little bit about her approach to examining witnesses, please.

Ms. Yona: "In examining witnesses, I learned to ask general questions so as to elicit details with powerful sensory associations: the colors, the sounds, the smells, that lodge an image in the mind and put the listener in the burning house."

Prof. Barry: Notice what's included in that list. Although she starts with colors and the sense of sight, she also adds the sense of hearing and the sense of smell. A little earlier in the book, she even highlights how a lawyer might use the sense of touch.

Ms. Yona: "Before you can engage the jurors' empathy, put them in the shoes of the accused or victim, make them feel the cold blade against their necks."

Prof. Barry: She never quite gets around to the sense of taste, but four out of five ain't bad—especially given that she sums up the section with a sentence that seems specifically designed for our class today. Read it for us, please.

Ms. Yona: "It is the particulars that make a story real."

Prof. Barry: Remember that sentence. Apply that sentence. Be, to the extent you can, *that* sentence.

Maybe someday it will even help earn you a seat on the Supreme Court.

19

Mary Karr and John Updike

Prof. Barry: Along with *My Beloved World* by Justice Sotomayor, there is another memoir that can help reinforce this idea of striving for five. Or I guess it's not so much a memoir as a book about memoirs. We mentioned it earlier today. It's called *The Art of Memoir* by Mary Karr. Here, Ms. Yona, is the advice she offers.

Ms. Yona: "In writing a scene, you must help the reader employ smell and taste and touch as well as image and noise."

Prof. Barry: Karr then adds some examples after suggesting that your writing should "brim over with the physical experiences that once streamed in."

Ms. Yona: "The smell of garlicky gumbo, your hand in an animal's fur, the ocean's phosphor lighting up bodies underwater all acid green."

Prof. Barry: See the range of senses she recommends? She ends with sight—"phosphor lighting up bodies underwater all acid green"—but she starts with smell and touch. She also offers, a little later on in the book, the following observation.

Ms. Yona: "A great detail feels particular in a way that argues for its truth."

Prof. Barry: Read that again. It's worth repeating.

Ms. Yona: "A great detail feels particular in a way that argues for its truth."

Prof. Barry: This gives us a way to understand what was so effective about the *How I Met Your Mother* detail we were talking about before, the one my law student used to describe his experience learning English. That detail feels particular in a way that argues for its truth. It gives the sentence a stamp of credibility. It garners trust.

Ms. Yona: Right.

Prof. Barry: Think about what it would mean if all your writing did that—if every cover letter you wrote garnered trust, if every essay you wrote garnered trust, if every email and memo to your boss convinced her of the value and reliability of what she was reading.

Decision-makers want this kind of writing. Judges, CEOs, admissions officers, venture capitalists—people in each of these positions need to get the sense that the documents on their desks were written by someone who knows what she is talking about. They need to be confident that you are fluent in your subject matter, that you understand and can communicate the nuances of a given issue, situation, or plan. And you know what demonstrates fluency, Ms. Yona?

Ms. Yona: What?

Prof. Barry: Details. Details demonstrate fluency. A legal brief is nothing without convincing, evocative details. An investment prospectus is nothing without convincing, evocative details. Same goes for position papers, personal statements, and business plans. If you want to persuade someone to take a specific action or adopt a certain point of view, you better have something vivid and concrete to get their attention.

Writer John Updike put this point well when explaining, back in 1984, his criteria for selecting that year's best American short stories.

Ms. Yona: "I want—perhaps we all want—facts . . . I can picture."

20

Facts I Can Picture

Prof. Barry: We'll often fall short of including all five senses in our writing. But John Updike's desire for "facts . . . I can picture" at least gives us a good starting point to work from, and there are few better models than Updike himself when it comes to crafting sentences that provide this kind of payoff. His words can make pictures even out of the most invisible of facts.

Take the sound of a voice, for example. In a first-class piece of sports writing called "Hub Fans Bid Adieu," Updike describes what it was like to hear Ted Williams thank the fans at Fenway Park during Williams's final game as a player back in September 1960. Please read it for us, Ms. Warsaw. We haven't yet heard from you today.

Ms. Warsaw: "[Williams] stooped to the microphone, and his voice sounded, after the others, very Californian; it seemed to be coming, excellently amplified, from a great distance, adolescently young and as smooth as butternut."

Prof. Barry: Or how about this passage from *Rabbit, Run*, the first in a series of novels Updike centered on the life of Harry "Rabbit" Angstrom, a former high school basketball star. Noticing a talented player much younger than he is, Rabbit reflects on his own path from teenage phenom to forgotten hero.

Ms. Warsaw: "You climb up through the little grades and then get to the top and everybody cheers; with the sweat in your eyebrows—"

Prof. Barry: Isn't "the sweat in your eyebrows" a great detail? Usually we read about sweat on somebody's forehead or sweat coming out of a person's pores. But Updike goes for something much more wonderfully particular.

Keep reading, please.

Ms. Warsaw: "With the sweat in your eyebrows you can't see very well and noise swirls around you and lifts you up, and then you're out, not forgotten at first, just out, and it feels good and cool and free."

Prof. Barry: A little more.

Ms. Warsaw: "You're out, and sort of melt, and keep lifting, until you become like to these kids just one more piece of the sky of adults that hangs over them in the town, a piece that for some queer reason has clouded and visited them. They've not forgotten [you]; worse, they've never heard of [you]."

Prof. Barry: In one of the later novels in the series, *Rabbit Redux*, Updike creates an even more vivid image of the fall from athletic grace that Rabbit, like all jocks, inevitably undergoes. After badly missing a jump shot in his backyard, Rabbit, now in middle age, turns to his thirteen-year-old son and says the following.

Ms. Warsaw: "It's a funny feeling when you get old. The brain sends out the order and the body looks the other way."

Prof. Barry: It is tough to imagine a better visual of fading physical ability than that.

Mr. Carlos (*jumping in*): That kind of reminds me of a T-shirt I once saw.

Prof. Barry: Yeah?

Mr. Carlos: I was at the gym back home.

Prof. Barry: Where's home?

Mr. Carlos: New Jersey. It was a YMCA, and the guy who was wearing the shirt was probably about sixty or seventy years old. You could tell he'd been slowing down the past couple of years, but he still looked like he was in really good shape.

Prof. Barry: Did he seem like he had a lot of "old man strength"?

Mr. Carlos: He seemed like he had *tons* of old man strength—and also a nice sense of humor, at least judging by the T-shirt.

Prof. Barry: What did it say?

Mr. Carlos: "The older I get, the better I was."

Prof. Barry: That's awesome. I don't think Updike could have put it better himself.

21

Updike, Oates, and Murakami

Ms. Bristol: So was Updike a big basketball fan or something?

Prof. Barry: You mean is that why he made Rabbit Angstrom a former player?

Ms. Bristol: Yeah.

Prof. Barry: He was actually a fan of a lot of sports. We already mentioned the baseball piece he wrote about Ted Williams. He also often wrote about golf, a sport he played regularly but never mastered. Referencing William Faulkner's *The Sound and the Fury*, Updike once wrote the following in an essay called "The Bliss of Golf."

Ms. Bristol: "Golf appeals to the idiot in us, and the child. What child does not grasp the pleasure-principle of miniature golf?"

Prof. Barry: Keep reading.

Ms. Bristol: "Just how childlike golf players become is proven by their frequent inability to count past five. There is a lovable injustice, a comic democracy, in the equality, for purposes of scoring, of a three-hundred-yard smash from an elevated tee and a three-inch tap-in. Or, let's not forget, a total whiff—the most comical stroke of all."

Prof. Barry: My favorite sentence comes next.

Ms. Bristol: "A ground-out in baseball or a tennis ball whapped into the net is not especially amusing; but bad shots in golf are endless fun—at least the other fellow's are."

Prof. Barry: Isn't that pretty good?

Ms. Bristol: Yeah.

Mr. Boh (*jumping in*)**:** Does Updike still play golf?

Prof. Barry: Nope. He died of lung cancer in 2009. But maybe there is some afterlife where he and other writer athletes could meet up for a round. Stephen Crane, who wrote the Civil War novel *The Red Badge of Courage*, was a standout baseball player at Syracuse University—even at one point claiming that as a catcher, he could grab, bare-handed, any pitch that was thrown at him.

There's also Ken Kesey, the author of *One Flew over the Cuckoo's Nest*. He was a star wrestler at the University of Oregon and eventually earned a spot as an alternative on the 1960 Olympic team.

Mr. Boh: Before or after he wrote *Cuckoo's Nest*?

Prof. Barry: Before. Another one is Jack Kerouac, who wrote *On the Road* and other Beat generation books, including *The Dharma Bums*, which the eyewear company Warby Parker hands out to each of its new employees on the first day of work—or at least did for a while.

Mr. Boh: What sport did Kerouac play?

Prof. Barry: Football, at Columbia—after turning down scholarship offers from Notre Dame and Boston College. But perhaps the most common sport for writers is running.

In an interview with the *Paris Review,* writer Don DeLillo, whose novel *Underworld* was nominated for the National Book Award, said his daily routine involves going for a run after he finishes his morning block of writing. He says it helps him "shake off one world and enter another." Joyce Carol Oates, whom we talked about earlier in the class, has said similar things about her own exercise regimen. Back in 1999, she wrote an essay for the *New York Times* under the title "To Invigorate Literary Mind, Start Moving Literary Feet." Here's the first line.

Mr. Boh: "Running!"

Prof. Barry: She seems pretty enthusiastic about the sport, doesn't she?

Mr. Boh: Yeah.

Prof. Barry: Later in the essay, she says that she can't think of any activity more exhilarating or nourishing to the imagination. Another world-class writer, Haruki Murakami, agrees. Perhaps the only person to win a fancy literary award like the Franz Kafka Prize and also complete an ultramarathon, Murakami published a book back in 2007 called *What I Talk about When I Talk about Running.* Here's what he says in it about his habit of running every day.

Mr. Boh: "People sometimes sneer at those who run every day, claiming they'll go to any length to live longer. But I don't think that's the reason most people run."

Prof. Barry: Keep reading.

Mr. Boh: "Most runners run not because they want to live longer, but because they want to live life to the fullest. If you're going to while away the years, it's far better to live them with clear goals and fully alive than in a fog, and I believe running helps you to do that."

Prof. Barry: And now the final bit.

Mr. Boh: "Exerting yourself to the fullest within your individual limits: that's the essence of running, and a metaphor for life—and for me, for writing as well. I believe many runners would agree."

22

Sedaris and Green

Prof. Barry: Of course, plenty of writers couldn't care less about sports. David Sedaris gives that impression of himself in "Go Carolina," a wonderful story he includes in one of his many best-selling books, *Me Talk Pretty One Day*. Why don't you read a little bit for us, Ms. Henrietta, to counter the more athletic-minded authors we just mentioned.

Ms. Henrietta: "I had no interest in football or basketball but had learned it was best to pretend otherwise. If a boy didn't care for barbecued chicken or potato chips, people would accept it as a matter of personal taste, saying, 'Oh well, I guess it takes all kinds.' You could turn up your nose at the president or Coke or even God, but there were names for boys who didn't like sports."

Prof. Barry: The narrator in the novel *Looking for Alaska* by John Green goes even further.

Ms. Henrietta: "I hated sports, and I hated people who played them, and I hated people who watched them, and I hated people who didn't hate people who watched or played them."

Prof. Barry: Side note: anyone recognize the writing move that appears in both the excerpt from Sedaris and the excerpt from Green? It involves conjunctions. We learned about it last class.

Mr. Dewey: The Gaiman Grab?

Prof. Barry: Right. The Gaiman Grab, or if you prefer the more technical term?

Mr. Dewey: Polysyndeton.

Prof. Barry: Exactly. Sedaris uses the move when he repeats the conjunction *or* in "You could turn up your nose at the president or Coke or even God." A non-Gaiman Grab version of that would be what, Mr. Dewey?

Mr. Dewey: "You could turn up your nose at the president, Coke, or even God."

Prof. Barry: Good. You simply remove the second *or*. As for the example from John Green, he could have written, "I hated sports, I hated people who played them, I hated people who watched them, and I hated people who didn't hate people who watched or played them." He could have, in other words, just separated the list with commas. But instead he included?

Mr. Dewey: An extra *and*.

Prof. Barry: More than just one extra.

Mr. Dewey: Right. Two extra.

Prof. Barry: Good. Read it for us again, please.

Mr. Dewey: "I hated sports, and I hated people who played them, and I hated people who watched them, and I hated people who didn't hate people who watched or played them."

Prof. Barry: I should say, however, that Green himself doesn't seem to share these views. He's a very public supporter of the English Premier League team Liverpool and has helped sponsor another team as well.

And although Sedaris isn't likely to join your fantasy football league or fill out a March Madness bracket anytime soon, it's not as if he's anti-exercise. In June 2014, he wrote a great essay for the *New Yorker* about his many adventures with his Fitbit. At times, he was apparently walking around twelve miles a day. Given that these miles were completed in England—where he lives with his partner of many years, the painter and set designer Hugh Hamrick—it seems worth mentioning that Charles Dickens sometimes hit the same amount in his daily jaunts.

Mr. Dewey: Dickens was a big walker?

Prof. Barry: Yeah. Same with Wallace Stevens, Virginia Woolf, and Henry David Thoreau. Thoreau wrote in an 1851 journal entry that "the moment my legs begin to move, my thoughts begin to flow."

He also believed that the kind of writing that comes from constantly sitting down is very dull to read. But let's return to the focus of today's class, the Power of the Particular, because we haven't yet considered something important: its moral dimensions.

23

The Poetics of Genocide

Prof. Barry: Do you mind helping us out with the moral dimensions of the Power of the Particular, Ms. Franzoni? You're our history major, right?

Ms. Franzoni: Yeah.

Prof. Barry: Good. Remember how in the first class we talked about some of the worst atrocities of the twentieth century: the Rwandan genocide, the Armenian genocide, the ethnic cleansing in Bosnia, and of course, the Holocaust?

Ms. Franzoni: Yeah.

Prof. Barry: All of those were aided by blanket generalizations about the terrorized groups. They were each fueled by the kind of pernicious stereotypes that turn unique, autonomous human beings into undifferentiated targets.

Ms. Franzoni: Right.

Prof. Barry: Rwandan Hutus didn't see the hundreds of thousands of Tutsis they killed in 1994 as having individual interests, aspirations, and personalities. They weren't encouraged to think about their victims' hobbies or family ties. Instead, they were encouraged to think what, Ms. Franzoni?

Ms. Franzoni: That every Tutsi was a cockroach.

Prof. Barry: And what do we do to cockroaches?

Ms. Franzoni: Exterminate them.

Prof. Barry: Same with lice, right? Remember that's what Nazis called Jewish people during World War II—lice.

Ms. Franzoni: Right.

Prof. Barry: How about maggots, flies, parasites, and rats? I ask because psychologist Steven Pinker has noted that each of these terms has been used by various perpetrators of genocide. Have you ever thought a maggot deserved a name, Ms. Franzoni? That it might have a soul and set of life goals?

Ms. Franzoni: No.

Prof. Barry: Have you ever stopped to consider what might be on its bucket list, what meaningful experiences it wants to have before the last of its days?

Ms. Franzoni: Definitely not.

Prof. Barry: Do you think that this lack of concern might make it easier to kill them without hesitation or remorse?

Ms. Franzoni: Probably.

Prof. Barry: A lot of folks agree with you—not just when it comes to actual maggots but also when it comes to people demonized *as* maggots. In *Less Than Human: Why We Demean, Enslave, and Exterminate Others*, philosopher David Livingstone Smith examines the process through which cruelty and genocide occur. He includes, for context, the opening statement of one of the prosecutors in the cases against Nazi doctors following World War II. Read it for us, please.

Ms. Franzoni: "The defendants in this case are charged with murders, tortures, and other atrocities committed in the name of medical science. The victims of these crimes are numbered in the hundreds of thousands."

Prof. Barry: Keep reading.

Ms. Franzoni: "A handful only are still alive; a few of the survivors will appear in this courtroom. But most of these miserable victims were slaughtered outright or died in the course of the tortures to which they were subjected."

Prof. Barry: Now comes the key point for our purposes.

Ms. Franzoni: "To their murderers, these wretched people were not individuals at all. They came in wholesale lots and were treated worse than animals."

Prof. Barry: Notice the prosecutor's wording: "They came in <u>wholesale lots</u>." They were not seen as "<u>individuals at all</u>." That's the poetics of genocide, a helpfully striking phrase for a terrible and way-too-common phenomenon.

Ms. Franzoni: Who came up with it?

Prof. Barry: Steven Pinker, the psychologist we referenced before. In a book called *The Better Angels of Our Nature*, Pinker identifies several atrocities that involve the dehumanizing move of referring to large groups of people not as individuals but as some kind of vermin or insect. A common label is to use the language of lice and nits.

Ms. Franzoni: What are nits?

Prof. Barry: They are the eggs that lice lay. Here's one of Pinker's examples.

Ms. Franzoni: "'Kill the nits and you will have no lice,' wrote an English commander in Ireland in 1641, justifying an order to kill thousands of Irish Catholics."

Prof. Barry: The next two focus on an often overlooked category of genocide victims: American Indians. We'll start with one from California in the 1850s.

Ms. Franzoni: "'A nit would make a louse,' recalled a Californian settler leader in 1856 before slaying 240 Yuki in revenge for their killing of a horse."

Prof. Barry: And now one from Colorado less than a decade later.

Ms. Franzoni: "'Nits make lice,' said Colonel John Chivington before the Sand Creek Massacre, which killed hundreds of Cheyenne and Arapaho in 1864."

Prof. Barry: As disturbing as these violent moments in history are, what's encouraging is that Pinker argues that they have actually become less frequent. The full title of his book is not just *The Better Angels of Our Nature*. The full title is *The Better Angels of Our Nature: Why Violence Has Declined*.

Here's one of the reasons he offers for the shift.

Ms. Franzoni: "Gentle Commerce."

Prof. Barry: Gentle Commerce is the idea that trade, particularly between nations, encourages cooperation and compromise, not violent conflict. Why engage in zero-sum warfare, this thinking goes, when you can engage in mutual exchange? In zero-sum warfare, one side dies. In mutual exchange, both sides end up with iPhones and Big Macs. Win-win trumps win-die.

Ms. Franzoni: What are some of the other reasons he gives?

Prof. Barry: The increasing influence of women. Women have historically been less violent than men. So the bigger part they play in both private and public decision-making, Pinker argues, the less violent society becomes.

A third reason fits in well with what we've been saying about the moral dimensions of the Power of the Particular, or at least the moral costs of not recognizing and valuing the individual humanity of people who are different than you. It's a lot easier to justify violent behavior when it's directed at people you identify as outsiders to your self-defined tribe, whether that tribe be familial, social, religious, or even intellectual. An insular "us-versus-them" approach to life can produce a dangerous combination of defensiveness and aggression.

Mr. Wild (*jumping in*)**:** Like the feud between the Grangerfords and the Shepherdsons in *Huck Finn*.

Prof. Barry: Exactly. The journalist Thomas Friedman uses that specific example in *From Beirut to Jerusalem*, his 1989 account of one of the most bitter feuds in modern history: the feud between Israel and Palestine.

Ms. Burke (*jumping in*)**:** So does Pinker not address that feud? Is that why he's so cheery about the state of violence in the world?

Prof. Barry: No. He addresses it. But he suggests that although major conflicts like that one still exist and other forms of tribal prejudice can certainly explode at any time, the overwhelming trend over the past few centuries has been toward cosmopolitanism and sympathetic perspective-taking. Here's what he writes earlier on in the book.

Ms. Burke: "The forces of cosmopolitanism such as literacy, mobility, and mass media can prompt people to take the perspectives of people unlike themselves and to expand their circle of sympathy to embrace them."

Prof. Barry: He then brings up, much later in the book, the research of Lynn Hunt, a historian at UCLA who has provided extensive evidence that the eighteenth-century rise of epistolary novels helped bring about a cultural shift toward both increased empathy for those who have suffered and an overall growth in humanitarianism.

Ms. Carroll (*jumping in*): What are epistolary novels?

Prof. Barry: They are novels that use personal letters to give readers direct access to a character's thoughts and feelings. If you've ever heard of Samuel Richardson's *Pamela* or *Clarissa,* those are both epistolary novels. So is *Lady Susan* by Jane Austen, *The Screwtape Letters* by C. S. Lewis, and *The Color Purple* by Alice Walker—though each of those was published long after the period Hunt focuses on. Here's how Pinker summarizes Hunt's findings. You want to read it for us?

Ms. Carroll: "Hunt suggests a causal chain: reading epistolary novels about characters unlike oneself exercises the ability to put oneself in other people's shoes, which turns one against cruel punishments and other abuses of human rights."

Prof. Barry: Pinker is careful to point out that the causation Hunt identifies may simply be correlation. But he nonetheless notes that the sequence of historical events supports her case. Read a little more, please, Ms. Carroll.

Ms. Carroll: "Technological advances in publishing, the mass production of books, the expansion of literacy, and the popularity of the novel all preceded the major humanitarian reforms of the 18th century."

Prof. Barry: Now the next sentence.

Ms. Carroll: "And in some cases a bestselling novel or memoir demonstrably exposed a wide range of readers to the suffering of a forgotten class of victims and led to a change in policy."

Prof. Barry: We've already mentioned one of the best sellers Pinker is referring to.

Ms. Carroll: Today?

Prof. Barry: No, during our first class, when we were talking about how writing is a superpower. Crafted by the daughter of a famous preacher, it outsold every other book in the nineteenth century—except the Bible. Anybody remember the name of it?

Ms. Franzoni (*jumping in*)**:** *Uncle Tom's Cabin* by Harriet Beecher Stowe.

Prof. Barry: Right. You know the name of the preacher?

Ms. Franzoni: Lyman Beecher?

Prof. Barry: That's right. Lyman Beecher. He was quite the celebrity, as was the author of two other works of fiction Pinker singles out. Here's a hint: during this person's tour of America in 1867, guards had to be stationed outside his hotel room to keep fans from mobbing him.

Ms. Franzoni: Alexis de Tocqueville?

Prof. Barry: No. Tocqueville visited America about forty-five years earlier and garnered much less public attention. He wasn't really famous at the time. He was simply sent here to study the prison system. Plus, I don't think he wrote fiction.

Ms. Yona (*jumping in*)**:** Didn't Oscar Wilde make a high-profile trip to America at some point?

Prof. Barry: He did, in 1882. And during that trip, he supposedly uttered what would be, if true, the single best response to a customs request ever. Asked if he had any goods to declare, Wilde replied, "I have nothing to declare—except my genius."

Ms. Yona: So is it him?

Prof. Barry: No. It's not him. It's actually someone who we just said sometimes walked up to twelve miles a day.

Ms. Yona: Charles Dickens?

Prof. Barry: Yeah. Pinker notes that two of Dickens's novels—*Oliver Twist* and *Nicholas Nickleby*—helped call attention to the mistreatment of children and the terrible conditions in orphanages and workhouses.

Pinker also mentions *To Kill a Mockingbird* by Harper Lee, which contains one of the most famous lines about empathy ever written in American literature. Anybody know it? Barack Obama quoted the line in his farewell address in 2016, right before the end of his second term as president.

Ms. Yona: Isn't it something about how you never really know a person until you walk in their shoes?

Prof. Barry: Close. Harper Lee—who, interestingly enough, said she did her best creative thinking while playing golf—takes the idea of walking in someone's shoes and makes it even more complete and visceral. She has Atticus Finch tell his daughter, Scout, "You never really understand a person until you consider things from his point of view—until you climb into his skin and walk around in it."

Ms. Yona: Right. "Climb into his skin." For some reason, I thought Lee stuck with the idea of shoes.

Prof. Barry: Shoes, skin, flip-flops, whatever. The point is that the line seems to really capture the importance and power of the kind of empathy Pinker describes. It's tough to imagine a better emblem of the "better angels of our nature" than Atticus Finch. He is the moral center of *To Kill a Mockingbird* and also a big reason many lawyers picked the profession they did. Ask your mom about him, Ms. Franzoni—you said in our first class that she's a lawyer, right?

Ms. Franzoni: Yeah.

Prof. Barry: Well, when you talk to her next, see what role, if any, Atticus Finch played in the way she thinks about what it means to be an attorney. Then ask her about another figure: a modern-day Atticus Finch named Bryan Stevenson. We're going to talk about him next.

24

Bryan Stevenson

Prof. Barry: When I say that Bryan Stevenson is a modern-day Atticus Finch, I'm simply echoing what other people have said about him, including the Pulitzer Prize–winning journalist Isabel Wilkerson. Here's the blurb she contributed to his book *Just Mercy*, which has been turned into a movie starring Michael B. Jordan, Jamie Foxx, and Brie Larson. Would you mind reading it for us, please, Mr. Marshall? I'm guessing you'll hear about Stevenson at least a few times when you head off to law school.

Mr. Marshall: "From the frontlines of social justice comes one of the most urgent voices of our era. Bryan Stevenson is a real-life, modern-day Atticus Finch who, through his work in redeeming innocent people condemned to death, has sought to redeem the country itself. This is a book of great power and courage. It is inspiring and suspenseful. A revelation."

Prof. Barry: John Grisham, the author of best sellers like *The Firm* and *The Pelican Brief*, used similar language in his own blurb for the book.

Mr. Marshall: "Not since Atticus Finch has a fearless and committed lawyer made such a difference in the American South. Though larger than life, Atticus exists only in fiction. Bryan Stevenson, however, is very much alive and doing God's work fighting for the poor, the oppressed, the voiceless, the vulnerable, the outcast, and those with no hope. *Just Mercy* is his inspiring and powerful story."

Prof. Barry: And then there is this bit of praise from Michelle Alexander, the acclaimed author and civil rights lawyer who wrote *The New Jim Crow: Mass Incarceration in the Age of Color Blindness.*

Mr. Marshall: "Bryan Stevenson is one of my personal heroes, perhaps the most inspiring and influential crusader for justice alive today, and *Just Mercy* is extraordinary. The stories told within these pages hold the potential to transform what we think we mean when we talk about justice."

Prof. Barry: Excitingly, one of my law students actually got the chance to intern at Stevenson's organization, the Equal Justice Initiative, down in Mobile, Alabama. The lawyers there have committed themselves to representing every death row inmate in the state. That's close to two hundred people.

Mr. Marshall: Is that the most in the country?

Prof. Barry: Per capita, yes. It's right ahead of Oklahoma and Mississippi. But before we get any deeper into the specific work Stevenson does, I want to introduce you to a wonderful essay by Binyavanga Wainaina, a Kenyan author who *Time* magazine once named in its annual list of the 100 Most Influential People in the World. The essay is called "How to Write about Africa." I think it helps us better understand what is so important—and so different—about Stevenson's approach to advocacy and criminal justice.

25

Unparticular

Prof. Barry: Wainaina wrote the essay we're going to look at for the literary magazine *Granta* back in 2005. It has since become perhaps the most read and shared piece in the publication's over 120-year history. A big reason: it's really funny.

Please read a sample of it for us, Mr. Farnoff. At this point in the essay, Wainaina is just beginning his satirical attack on the ugly and inaccurate stereotypes many rely on when writing about Africa. His advice is meant to be taken in the same spirit as Jonathan Swift's *A Modest Proposal* and clips from the *Daily Show*.

Mr. Farnoff: "Never have a picture of a well-adjusted African on the cover of your book, or in it, unless that African has won the Nobel Prize. An AK-47, prominent ribs, naked breasts: use these. If you must include an African, make sure you get one in Masai or Zulu or Dogon dress."

Prof. Barry: Keep going.

Mr. Farnoff: "In your text, treat Africa as if it were one country. It is hot and dusty with rolling grasslands and huge herds of animals and tall, thin people who are starving. Or it is hot and steamy with very short people who eat primates. Don't get bogged down with precise descriptions."

Prof. Barry: "Don't get bogged down with precise descriptions." I love that. It's such a great way to highlight just how important precise descriptions actually are, especially when writing or talking about a topic as vulnerable to pernicious generalizations as Africa. The next couple lines reinforce this point. They also, at the end, give us a really helpful bit of vocabulary: *unparticular*.

Mr. Farnoff: "Africa is big: fifty-four countries, [more than a billion] people who are too busy starving and dying and warring and emigrating to read your book. The continent is full of deserts, jungles, highlands, savannahs, and many other things, but your reader doesn't care about all that, so keep your descriptions romantic and evocative and unparticular."

Prof. Barry: What I think is so helpful about the term *unparticular* is Wainaina's deliberate use of the prefix *un*- to form the word. Imagine if he had instead written the sentence using the word *general*.

Mr. Farnoff: "So keep your descriptions romantic and evocative and general."

Prof. Barry: That's not as powerful, is it? Even though, of course, saying something is *general* is the same as saying something is *unparticular*.

Mr. Farnoff: Right.

Prof. Barry: Say a little more about the difference.

Mr. Farnoff: The *un*- definitely makes *unparticular* stand out more.

Prof. Barry: How?

Mr. Farnoff: Because you don't really see *un*- in front of many words, or at least not in front of that word.

Prof. Barry: You're used to seeing it in front of words like *believable*, right? To form?

Mr. Farnoff: *Unbelievable.*

Prof. Barry: Or in front of the word *expected* to form?

Mr. Farnoff: *Unexpected.*

Prof. Barry: Good. Both of those are common enough terms that you don't really notice when they appear in print or come out of somebody's mouth. But with *unparticular*?

Mr. Farnoff: *That* you're gonna notice.

Prof. Barry: Right. Sort of like *uncola*, which the soft drink 7UP included in its marketing materials for more than two decades. Or *un-carrier*, which cellular company T-Mobile used at various points. Or even *unwich*—anybody know which sandwich company came up with that phrase to distinguish its menu from more standard shops?

Ms. Bart (*jumping in***):** Isn't that Jimmy John's?

Prof. Barry: Yup. Head to the Jimmy John's on State Street after class today. You should see an *unwich* listed on the menu. I think they may have even registered it as a trademark.

Ms. Bart: Really?

Prof. Barry: Yeah. But businesses aren't the only ones to use the *un*-move. The English novelist and poet Thomas Hardy—whose books include *Far from the Maddening Crowd*, *Tess of the d'Urbervilles*, and *Jude the Obscure*—was particularly fond of it, as one of the teachers in Alan Bennett's Tony Award–winning play *The History Boys* explains. Read the passage for us, please, Ms. Bart.

Ms. Bart: "'Uncoffined' is a typical Hardy usage. A compound adjective formed by putting 'un-' in front of the noun. Or verb, of course. Un-kissed. Un-rejoicing. Un-confessed. Un-embraced."

Prof. Barry: The teacher then says that the poet Philip Larkin, who admired Hardy immensely, uses it in words like *un-spent* and *un-fingermarked*.

My favorite example, however, comes from *TransAtlantic*, a novel by Colum McCann that explores, among other things, what it might have been like for escaped slave Frederick Douglass when he toured Ireland in the 1840s. Here's how one of the characters, a Kenyan-born literary scholar named David Manyaki, describes the effect of the trip on Douglass.

Ms. Bart: "He went back to America unslaved."

Prof. Barry: To which his conversation partner responds, if only internally?

Ms. Bart: "*Unslaved*. It was a curious and lovely word, and I liked Manyaki all the more for it."

Prof. Barry: I feel the same way about Binyavanga Wainaina's use of the word *unparticular* in the essay about Africa we've been looking at. It is a curious and lovely word—and I like Wainaina all the more for using it.

26

Africa Africa

Prof. Barry: Wainaina's use of the word *unparticular* is not just lovely and curious; it's also morally important, at least in the context of the essay. The word helps expose the troubling way the individual humanity and specific experiences of Africans are often ignored and a whole continent of people, where more than two thousand languages are spoken, is reduced to a single pitiable mass. A joke by the comedian Trevor Noah, who grew up in South Africa and speaks four languages himself, highlights this tendency. You want to help me tell it, Mr. Farnoff? You said last class that you are a fan of comedians.

Mr. Farnoff: Sure.

Prof. Barry: The joke comes at the beginning of a 2011 documentary called *You Laugh But It's True*, which was shot years before Noah became a big star and succeeded Jon Stewart as the host of the *Daily Show*. In the scene, he is onstage at a comedy club, sharing a conversation he recently had in an airport with what sounds like a very annoying and ignorant American teenage girl. Noticing his accent, the girl says the following.

Mr. Farnoff: "Oh my gaawd. You talk funny."

Prof. Barry: To which Noah responds?

Mr. Farnoff: "Excuse me?"

Prof. Barry: So the teenager repeats herself and then asks a question.

Mr. Farnoff: "Yeah, you talk funny. Where are you from?"

Prof. Barry: Noah then tells her, very politely.

Mr. Farnoff: "I am from South Africa."

Prof. Barry: The teenager can't believe it.

Mr. Farnoff: "Oh my gaawd. Like Africa?"

Prof. Barry: Noah remains polite.

Mr. Farnoff: "Yes."

Prof. Barry: The teenager keeps going.

Mr. Farnoff: "Like *Africa* Africa?"

Prof. Barry: Which leads to the punchline of the story. Noah, at once charming and merciless, responds to the girl's question this way.

Mr. Farnoff: "No. The one next to it."

27
Just Mercy

Prof. Barry: Part of the reason I brought up Trevor Noah's anecdote about South Africa is because it gives us a way to return to Bryan Stevenson. Any chance someone knows who else Stevenson has been compared to, in addition to Atticus Finch?

Here's a hint: the person may be the most famous South African in history, and he is certainly one of the most famous leaders of the twentieth century. Plus, he was featured in a great *30 for 30* documentary by ESPN about rugby. It's called *The 16th Man*.

Ms. Burke: Nelson Mandela?

Prof. Barry: Yup. Here's how *New York Times* columnist Nicholas Kristof articulated the comparison back in 2014.

Ms. Burke: "Bryan Stevenson may, indeed, be America's Mandela."

Prof. Barry: Those words now appear on the back cover of the paperback version of Stevenson's book *Just Mercy*. And tucked inside, among a bunch of other endorsements—including ones by the *Financial Times*, the *Philadelphia Inquirer*, and the *Boston Globe*—you'll find similar praise by someone who worked closely with Mandela: Archbishop Desmond Tutu, the recipient of the 1984 Nobel Peace Prize.

Read it for us, please.

Ms. Burke: "Bryan Stevenson is America's young Nelson Mandela, a brilliant lawyer fighting with courage and conviction to guarantee justice for all."

Prof. Barry: One thing that makes Stevenson deserving of all this praise is his expert use of the Power of the Particular. He has a real knack for humanizing people who might otherwise be written off as irredeemable criminals. Here is one of *Just Mercy*'s most frequently repeated lines.

Ms. Burke: "Each of us is more than the worst thing we've ever done."

Prof. Barry: Isn't that great? The statement is such a helpful bulwark against our habit of demonizing people who have made a mistake, of reducing them to a single action or label without first understanding the circumstances of their lives and the many dimensions of their personalities. "We have all hurt someone and have been hurt," Stevenson writes, reflecting on the execution of Jimmy Dill, an intellectually disabled man who was charged with murdering someone whose true cause of death may have been inept medical care. Please read the follow-up sentences.

Ms. Burke: "We all share the condition of brokenness even if our brokenness is not equivalent. I desperately wanted mercy for Jimmy Dill and would have done anything to create justice for him, but I couldn't pretend that his struggle was disconnected from my own."

Prof. Barry: Keep going.

Ms. Burke: "The ways in which I have been hurt—and have hurt others—are different from the ways Jimmy Dill suffered and caused suffering. But our shared brokenness connected us."

Prof. Barry: Stevenson's moving account of Dill's plight and debilitating stutter as well as the touching way Dill calls Stevenson on the phone to thank him hours before being put to death—all this is actually surpassed by the story Stevenson tells about George Mitchell, the wrongly convicted timber cutter around which much of *Just Mercy* is built.

Technique-wise, it's really the prototypical Power of the Particular move: take one especially compelling case and use it to comment on a much wider set of issues and events. Adrian Nicole Leblanc uses this technique in *Random Family*, her in-depth look at poverty in the South Bronx. Andrea Elliot uses it in "Invisible Child," her multipart magazine series on homeless children. And so does Dave Eggers in *Zeitoun*, which chronicles both Hurricane Katrina and the risks of trying to be a good citizen in America when your first name is Abdulrahman.

Ms. Maat (*jumping in*): We were assigned *Zeitoun* in my class on environmental disasters.

Prof. Barry: Did you like it?

Ms. Maat: A lot. It reads like a novel.

Prof. Barry: You think so?

Ms. Maat: Yeah. I actually didn't know it was a true story until one of my friends told me.

Prof. Barry: That's pretty funny. *Zeitoun* is a good example of the benefits that can come when a literary sensibility—Eggers has written a lot of fiction as well—experiments with nonfiction.

That said, some of the best examples of this more structural use of the Power of the Particular, where something seemingly minute is used to communicate a broad range of ideas and meanings, *are* works of fiction. Several of the writers we've already talked about today have quite famously organized entire books around a single day. James Joyce is one. Do you remember, Mr. Wild, which one of his novels takes place over the course of just twenty-four hours?

Mr. Wild: *Ulysses*?

Prof. Barry: Yeah. Joyce's *Ulysses* is one day in the life of the character Leopold Bloom. Any idea which day?

Mr. Wild: Wednesday?

Prof. Barry: I'm actually looking for a date rather than a day of the week.

Mr. Wild: I don't think I know the date.

Prof. Barry: That's okay. I can tell you. It's June 16, 1904. Any guesses why Joyce picked it?

Mr. Wild: It was his birthday?

Prof. Barry: Nope. Joyce's birthday is February 2nd. He picked June 16, 1904, for a more romantic reason.

Mr. Wild: That's the day he met his wife?

Prof. Barry: Close. That's the day they went on their first date.

28

Alliteration

Prof. Barry: The date Joyce picked for *Ulysses* reminds us to be aware of the creative choices in the books, movies, and other media we encounter. Dates, settings, character names—all these reflect deliberate decisions.

Or think about the names of sports teams. What, for example, do you notice is the same about each of the following names: the Pittsburgh Pirates, the Jacksonville Jaguars, and the Cleveland Cavaliers?

Mr. Wild: They all use alliteration.

Prof. Barry: Just like the Boston Bruins and the Seattle Seahawks, right?

Mr. Wild: Right.

Prof. Barry: Or the Columbus Crew and the Buffalo Bills?

Mr. Wild: Yeah.

Prof. Barry: And it's not just professional sports where we see this, is it? For example, every spring the world of college basketball is taken over not by "March Craziness" but by?

Mr. Wild: March Madness.

Prof. Barry: And if, say, Michigan makes it to the last weekend of March Madness, we don't say they've made it to the "Final Group." Instead, we say they've made it to?

Mr. Wild: The Final Four.

Prof. Barry: But to be included in the Final Four, you first need to win your game in the previous round, which is made up of eight teams. What's that round called—not the "Fantastic Eight" but the?

Mr. Wild: Elite Eight.

Prof. Barry: And even before winning your game in the Elite Eight, you have to win your game in a round that could be called the "Amazing Sixteen."

Mr. Wild: Right.

Prof. Barry: But what's that round really called?

Mr. Wild: The Sweet Sixteen.

Prof. Barry: All of which points to one conclusion.

Mr. Wild: What?

Prof. Barry: Someone at the NCAA must have been an English major.

29

Why Is It This Way Instead of Some Other Way?

Prof. Barry: I joke about alliteration, but it can actually be a helpful way to highlight a question you can ask about any piece of writing. Please read it for us, Ms. Nina.

Ms. Nina: "Why is it this way instead of some other way?"

Prof. Barry: You can ask that question about a poem. You can ask it about a billboard. You can ask it about a letter, column, or lease.

And you can also ask it of a lot of things that aren't writing. Paintings. Engines. Cakes. Floral decorations. Anything created, anything arranged, anything put together could—the question reminds us—be put together differently. There is choice involved. There is a mind at work.

Ms. Nina: Right.

Prof. Barry: What I love about alliteration is the way it calls attention to this fact. *Pride and Prejudice* didn't have to be called *Pride and Prejudice*; Jane Austen could have kept the original title.

Ms. Nina: Which was?

Prof. Barry: *First Impressions.* Nor did *Sense and Sensibility* have to be called *Sense and Sensibility*. The title Austen started with was *Elinore and Marianne*. Just like one of the titles F. Scott Fitzgerald started with when writing *The Great Gatsby* was the following. Read it for us, please.

Ms. Nina: *Among the Ash Heap and the Millionaires.*

Prof. Barry: He also considered these next two.

Ms. Nina: *Trimalchio in West Egg.*

Prof. Barry: And?

Ms. Nina: *The High-Bouncing Lover.*

Prof. Barry: It was actually Fitzgerald's wife, Zelda, or maybe his editor, Max Perkins—or maybe both—who convinced him to go with *The Great Gatsby*.

But whoever deserves credit, the pairing of *great* with *Gatsby* was clearly deliberate. The book is not *The Wonderful Gatsby*. Nor is it called *The Amazing Gatsby*. It's called *The Great Gatsby*. The rhythm and sound of that double *g* give the book an added charm.

Don't get me wrong, though. We already said that excessive alliteration can really irk people. Which is why whenever we are thinking about using it, we need to keep in mind another important writerly quality: restraint.

30

Restraint

Prof. Barry: To help us understand the importance of restraint, let's begin with an Irish writer who might have benefited from more of it. Her name is Amanda McKittrick Ros, and she once earned this headline from the *Daily Telegraph* in Britain: "Awful Author Addicted to Alliteration Achieves Acclaim Again." The article includes a sample from Ros's first novel, *Irene Iddesleigh*. Would you please read it for us, Ms. Cawlow? I've underlined all the bits of alliteration.

Ms. Cawlow: "The living sometimes learn the touchy tricks of the traitor, the tardy and the tempted; the dead have evaded the flighty earthy future, and form to swell the retinue of retired rights, the righteous school of the invisible and the rebellious roar of the raging nothing."

Prof. Barry: Her other two novels have similarly alliterative titles—*Delina Delaney* and *Helen Huddleson*—as do two of her books of poetry, *Poems of Puncture* and *Forms of Formation*. After reading them, you might understand why the entry for Ros in the *Oxford Companion to Irish Literature* says the following.

Ms. Cawlow: "Uniquely dreadful."

Prof. Barry: You might also understand why I'm now stressing restraint. Particularly as you acquire more writing tips and techniques, you need to know when to hold back a little and resist the pull of literary pyrotechnics. Just because you know how to dribble behind your back doesn't mean you should.

Ms. Toth (*jumping in*): "Kill your darlings." That's what my creative writing teachers always say. If you start falling in love with your own words, you're done for.

Prof. Barry: I don't know. I've always thought the "kill your darlings" advice was a bit misguided. I realize a bunch of great writers have been associated with it, including William Faulkner and Eudora Welty, and I remember Stephen King emphasizing the point in that great book *On Writing* we've mentioned a few times. But part of me thinks, "You know, creating phrases and sentences you're proud of is really hard. So when that minimiracle happens, murder shouldn't necessarily be your first impulse."

Ms. Toth: So you don't believe in killing your darlings.

Prof. Barry: Not as strongly as other people seem to. That said, I think King in particular is right to highlight the at times self-indulgent quality of a lot of writing—the way the reader seems to get pushed out of the way and replaced by the writer's own ego. This is a paraphrase, but when King repeats the "kill your darlings" mantra in his book, he directly targets a certain kind of narcissism. "Kill your darlings," he says. "Kill your darlings. Even when it breaks your egocentric little heart. Kill your darlings."

It's sort of like an observation the journalist Ben Yagoda makes in another book on writing, *The Sound on the Page*: "Writers who are unaware of or uninterested in readers are like people who do not look at you when they're speaking to you."

If you're going to use alliteration or any other writing move, it should be with the reader in mind. Will this construction help my audience better understand and remember what I'm trying to communicate? Will it inform them? Will it persuade them? Will it entertain or improve them? If not, sure: kill your darlings. A darling without a specific purpose is not much of a darling at all.

31
The Big Dig

Prof. Barry: What I want to do now is give you a sense of how these choices play out when you're actually putting a piece of writing together. We can take as an example a textbook I got to help out with back when I was in graduate school.

Ms. Henrietta (*jumping in*)**:** What was it on?

Prof. Barry: Human trafficking.

Ms. Henrietta: Really?

Prof. Barry: I know—not exactly the cheeriest of topics. But it's an area of law I'm really interested in, and the opportunity came with the chance to work with four of the top human trafficking lawyers in the country.

Ms. Henrietta: How long did it take you all to finish?

Prof. Barry: Longer than any of us ever anticipated. Which seems common for ambitious projects.

Remember Daniel Kahneman from earlier today and also from our first class? He's the psychologist who won the Nobel Prize in economics and included that great example of "Italy won" versus "France lost" in his book *Thinking, Fast and Slow*.

Ms. Henrietta: Yeah.

Prof. Barry: Well, Kahneman talks in that book about something called the "planning fallacy." It's the tendency people have to underestimate the time it will take them to complete a task, especially a big task like writing a book or remodeling a house. Or in the case of the city of Boston, the "Big Dig." Anybody know what that is? Is anybody in here actually from Boston?

(*No hands go up*)

How about New England more generally?

Mr. Dewey: I'm from Vermont.

Prof. Barry: Close enough—especially if you've heard of the Big Dig. Have you?

Mr. Dewey: Wasn't it some big construction project?

Prof. Barry: Yup. One of the biggest ever done on the US highway system. The physical work began in 1991 and was supposed to be completed in about seven years. But that didn't happen, did it?

Mr. Dewey: No.

Prof. Barry: You know how long it eventually took?

Mr. Dewey: Something like twice as long as they thought, right?

Prof. Barry: Right. The initial estimates were off not just by a couple months or even a couple years—they were off by close to a decade.

And the cost? The cost was off by billions of dollars. Not millions—*billions*. The original projection was around $3 billion. You know what the final price tag was?

Mr. Dewey: $5 billion?

Prof. Barry: Triple that.

Mr. Dewey: Really? $15 billion?

Prof. Barry: Yup. And if you factor in the interest payments on the debt incurred, the price was actually closer to $24 billion, according to the *Boston Globe*. That's a pretty expensive miscalculation.

32

The Planning Fallacy

Prof. Barry: The Big Dig is an extreme case of the planning fallacy. And although the example Kahneman gives in *Thinking, Fast and Slow* isn't nearly as dramatic, it's in some ways even more instructive given that it involves a bunch of psychologists who probably should have known better. Here's what happened.

When Kahneman was a young academic back in Israel, he was asked to head a team of researchers brought together to design a new curriculum for the country's high schools. A year into the project, he asked everyone how long they thought it would take to finish.

Mr. Dewey: What did they say?

Prof. Barry: "About two years." Any guess on how long it actually took?

Mr. Dewey: A lot more than two years.

Prof. Barry: Yup. It took close to eight.

Mr. Dewey: Seriously?

Prof. Barry: Seriously. By the time Kahneman and his coauthors turned in their manuscript, the Israeli government was no longer interested. Which means the curriculum they put together was never used.

Mr. Dewey: That sucks.

Prof. Barry: Fortunately, a similar thing didn't happen with that human trafficking textbook I mentioned. But there were moments when we were so behind schedule that I was reminded of a quip by Douglas Adams, the author of *The Hitchhiker's Guide to the Galaxy*. Read it for us, please, Mr. Dewey.

Mr. Dewey: "I love deadlines. I love the whooshing noise they make as they go by."

33

It's All About *We*

Prof. Barry: In addition to highlighting the planning fallacy, bringing up the human trafficking textbook gives us a chance to apply some of what we've been learning in this course about word choice, framing, and using particular details. Would you mind reading the opening two sentences of the book for us, please, Mr. Marshall?

Mr. Marshall: "Labor trafficking touches many aspects of our daily lives. It touches, through supply chains, the T-shirts we wear, the cell phones we use, and the chocolate we eat and share with others."

Prof. Barry: Any thoughts on why the authors decided to open with a couple of sentences on labor trafficking? Why do you think they focused the reader's attention on that form of trafficking rather than on sex trafficking?

Mr. Marshall: Is that form of trafficking more common?

Prof. Barry: Yup. But for a lot of people, when they think of human trafficking, they think of sex trafficking. They think of the movie *Taken*.

Mr. Marshall: With Liam Neeson?

Prof. Barry: Yeah. Who gets trafficked in that movie?

Mr. Marshall: His daughter—a rich white girl.

Prof. Barry: On?

Mr. Marshall: A vacation in Paris.

Prof. Barry: You think that happens a lot?

Mr. Marshall: Probably not.

Prof. Barry: Right. That said, I had a good time watching *Taken* when it first came out. And if Liam Neeson's character wants to bring his special set of skills to the Human Trafficking Clinic here at Michigan, I'd be happy to write him a recommendation letter.

But as far as educating future lawyers through a textbook goes, it seemed important to lead with a more realistic picture of the trafficking landscape. It also seemed important not to come across as self-righteous, which is a real danger when it comes to this kind of work.

Mr. Marshall: Right.

Prof. Barry: Notice, for example, the pronouns the authors chose for the sentences you read. They didn't write that labor trafficking touches the "T-shirts you wear, the cell phones you use, and the chocolate you eat and share with others." Instead, they wrote what?

Mr. Marshall: Labor trafficking touches the "T-shirts we wear, the cell phones we use, and the chocolate we eat and share with others."

Prof. Barry: Why do you think they made that choice? Why do you think they went with *we* instead of *you*?

Mr. Marshall: Because *you* seems too accusatory. Like you're trying to shame the readers.

Prof. Barry: Good. What's better about using *we*?

Mr. Marshall: *We* gives the sense that human trafficking is a problem that everybody, including the authors, is in some sense responsible for.

Prof. Barry: Through?

Mr. Marshall: The products we all own.

Prof. Barry: Right. And let's be clear: while the authors and I were putting this book together, we did wear T-shirts, we did use cell phones, and we certainly did eat chocolate.

The authors wrote the book not because they are morally superior to everyone when it comes to human trafficking; they wrote the book because they want to teach people about the various dimensions of the problem and offer concrete ways to address it. Adopting the perspective of *we*, focusing the point of view in that way, seemed to align well with what they ultimately wanted to communicate. It's a great example of the "framing" we did in our first class.

It also now sets us up to further explore what we've been learning today: using compelling details and the Power of the Particular.

34

Cherry Tomatoes

Prof. Barry: Let's have you read those first two sentences of the human trafficking textbook again, Mr. Marshall. There's more to notice.

Mr. Marshall: "Labor trafficking touches many aspects of our daily lives. It touches, through supply chains, the T-shirts we wear, the cell phones we use, and the chocolate we eat and share with others."

Prof. Barry: Good. Now read this version.

Mr. Marshall: "Labor trafficking touches many aspects of our daily lives. It touches, through supply chains, many of the products we use."

Prof. Barry: What's better about the first version?

Mr. Marshall: It's more specific.

Prof. Barry: Do you think some people might actually be wearing a T-shirt when they read those sentences?

Mr. Marshall: Probably.

Prof. Barry: And maybe have their cell phones or some chocolate nearby?

Mr. Marshall: Yeah.

Prof. Barry: Me too. But let's spend a little more time on that chocolate part. Suppose that instead of chocolate, the authors had said cherry tomatoes. Suppose the sentences read, "Labor trafficking touches many aspects of our daily lives. It touches, through supply chains, the T-shirts we wear, the cell phones we use, and the <u>cherry tomatoes</u> we eat and share with others."

Mr. Marshall: I don't know. That might be a little *too* particular.

Prof. Barry: What do you mean?

Mr. Marshall: I mean, I get chocolate. Everyone eats and shares chocolate. But I'm not sure everyone eats and shares cherry tomatoes. I'm not sure everybody has even heard of cherry tomatoes.

Prof. Barry: Cherry tomatoes would have targeted too small of an audience?

Mr. Marshall: Yeah. Way too small.

Prof. Barry: And maybe alienated some people, or at least communicated an off-putting elitism?

Mr. Marshall: Exactly.

Prof. Barry: Well, the authors agreed with you. Like a dummy, I originally suggested we go with cherry tomatoes. But fortunately, they were all wise enough to see that as a bad move. One, the former attorney general of New Jersey, wrote me this long, hilarious email outlining the errors of my ways.

Mr. Marshall: How did you respond?

Prof. Barry: In the only way that was reasonable: with total agreement. Even after reading just a few lines of her email, I quickly realized how wrong I was. Cherry tomatoes were, as you said, too particular.

That can be a real danger when trying to create memorable images, which is certainly something I thought a lot about when I helped shape the next sentence in the book. Read it for us, please. It introduces sex trafficking.

Mr. Marshall: "Sex trafficking intertwines with much of the global sex industry, whether through the sale of young males into brothels in Bangalore, the sale of young females into strip clubs in San Diego, or the forced prostitution of both males and females, of all ages, in states across the country and countries across the world."

Prof. Barry: Notice how the authors picked one city outside the US (Bangalore) and one inside the US (San Diego). Why do you think they did that? Why do you think they didn't go with "brothels in Bangalore" and "strip clubs in Saigon"?

Mr. Marshall: They probably wanted to stress that sex trafficking is an American problem too.

Prof. Barry: Good. Just like they wanted to stress that it is also a problem that isn't limited to a specific gender or age. Men get trafficked. Women get trafficked. Teenagers get trafficked. Toddlers, horrifyingly, get trafficked. And so do people who should be enjoying their golden years. Right around the time the book came out, there was a raid on a trafficking ring here in Detroit. One of the victims interviewed was in her fifties.

Mr. Marshall: For sex trafficking?

Prof. Barry: Yeah. The raid was on a massage parlor. But let's return for a moment to the choice to use Bangalore and San Diego as examples. Each city highlights an important aspect of the Power of the Particular that we are about to focus on more closely: you can vary its specificity.

35
Google Maps

Prof. Barry: One way to understand the range of specificity you have at your disposal when using the Power of the Particular is to think about Google Maps. Is it safe to assume you have used Google Maps, Ms. Bart?

Ms. Bart: Yeah. I use it all the time.

Prof. Barry: Good. You know those icons at the bottom of the screen, the ones that let you zoom in and out of whatever you are looking at?

Ms. Bart: Yeah.

Prof. Barry: Well, you have the same sort of freedom with the Power of the Particular. Take Bangalore, the city paired with brothels in the textbook's first example of sex trafficking. The authors could have zoomed the specificity out a little bit and written "brothels in India," right?

Ms. Bart: Right.

Prof. Barry: They could have also zoomed it out a lot and written "brothels in Asia." Or zoomed it out even more and written "brothels in the Eastern Hemisphere."

Ms. Bart: Yeah.

Prof. Barry: Or if they wanted to go in the opposite direction—perhaps with the example of San Diego—they could have zoomed in instead of zooming out. They could have written not "strip clubs in San Diego" but "strip clubs off Route 163," which is a highway that runs through San Diego. Or they could have picked a specific strip club in San Diego. You have that option with the Power of the Particular. You can get pretty granular.

Ms. Bart: Can you get too granular?

Prof. Barry: Definitely. Imagine if the authors had chosen not San Diego but some individual building, or neighborhood, or road. What's the problem with being that specific?

Ms. Bart: People might not know what you're talking about. They might not recognize the reference point.

Prof. Barry: Exactly. So we need to be careful as we toggle back and forth between the general and the specific. We need to develop, I think, a bit of nuance.

To help with that, we're now going to close class today with something we will return to throughout the semester: "Notes on Nuance."

36

Notes on Nuance

Prof. Barry: What I mean by Notes on Nuance are some suggestions for how you can enhance your writing with additional levels of subtlety and style. We'll try to make time for this at the end of each class from now on. It'll give us a chance to play around with a whole series of writing moves that, even if they don't merit a whole class period, might be fun for you to try out. The first one comes from a novel we talked about last week, *The Art of Fielding* by Chad Harbach.

Ms. Bristol (*jumping in*): The one about the shortstop?

Prof. Barry: Yeah. Check out how Harbach uses the word *almost* in the following sentence. He's describing the effortless way the shortstop played his position.

Ms. Bristol: "Even at full speed his face looked bland, <u>almost</u> bored, like that of a virtuoso practicing scales."

Prof. Barry: Or how about this next sentence from a writer who grew up here in Michigan and then went on to win the 2003 Pulitzer Prize in fiction. His name is Jeffrey Eugenides, and in the example, he's trying to communicate how badly one of the characters in his novel *The Marriage Plot* smelled after a late night of smoky, sticky partying.

Ms. Bristol: "Madeleine's need for a shower was extreme, almost medical."

Prof. Barry: See how the move works? You use *almost* to pair one word, *extreme*, with a slightly more exaggerated alternative, *medical*.

Ms. Bristol: Right.

Prof. Barry: To show you that it's not just fiction writers like Eugenides and Harbach who do this, here is the historian Karen Armstrong relying on the move to help her identify how the theological approach of Franciscan philosopher John Duns Scotus differed from his thirteenth-century contemporaries.

Ms. Bristol: "Scotus's preference for a natural, almost scientifically based theology reflected a fundamental change in the training of theologians."

Prof. Barry: Now one from the world of science. It appears in *The Gene: An Intimate History* by the oncologist Siddhartha Mukherjee. He's quoting George Huntington, the doctor who discovered the ailment now known as Huntington's disease.

Ms. Bristol: "We suddenly came upon two women, mother and daughter, both tall, thin, almost cadaverous, both bowing, twisting, grimacing."

Prof. Barry: See how *almost* works there? It gives Huntington—and by extension, Mukherjee—a chance to express a helpful amount of precision and gradation. The mother and daughter were close to looking cadaverous, close to looking dead, but they weren't quite there yet.

Ms. Bristol: Right.

Prof. Barry: Or take the previous example about John Duns Scotus. He had a preference for something very similar to a scientifically based theology—"a natural, almost scientifically based theology"—but it wasn't *exactly* a scientifically based theology.

Ms. Maat (*jumping in*): Do you have any more?

Prof. Barry: Any more what?

Ms. Maat: Any more of these little writing moves.

Prof. Barry: You like them?

Ms. Maat: Yeah. A lot.

Prof. Barry: Good. They're fun. And useful. I mean, you shouldn't try to use this *almost* move in every sentence you write. But once in a while, it can create a neat effect. Same with this next one, which will be the last move for the day. It works kind of like the *almost* move, except this time with the word *even*. You can see it in a sentence from the Irish writer Roddy Doyle. He's describing the stylish sunglasses worn by a famous Dutch soccer player named Edgar Davids.

Ms. Maat: "On Edgar Davids, they looked impressive, terrifying, even sexy."

Prof. Barry: Or how about this example from *Too Much Happiness* by Alice Munro, the Nobel Prize winner we brought up when discussing the way great writers both show and tell.

Ms. Maat: "My mother had a habit of hanging on to—even treasuring—the foibles of my distant infantile state."

Prof. Barry: The dash there really highlights the effect, though you can certainly get by with just a comma. Here's the Historian T. J. Stiles choosing the comma options in his award-winning biography of shipping titan Cornelius Vanderbilt.

Ms. Maat: "Perhaps there were those who understood that Vanderbilt's true significance was more complex, even contradictory."

Prof. Barry: We'll close, however, with two examples from Mark Twain. The first comes at the end of a story called "Punch, Brothers, Punch."

Ms. Maat: "It was for a worthy, even a noble, purpose."

Prof. Barry: The second comes toward the middle of a different story, "The $30,000 Bequest."

Ms. Maat: "Sally was willing, even anxious, to do it."

Prof. Barry: I hope you're starting to notice something from these and all the other examples we've talked about: writing doesn't have to be this magically foreign process. Mark Twain, Alice Munro, Karen Armstrong, Roddy Doyle—sure, these people have talent; sure, they have unique literary sensibilities and distinctive points of view. But they also have identifiable techniques for putting sentences together, techniques we can study and practice ourselves.

To give us a slightly different perspective, let's turn for a moment to illustrator Andrew Loomis and his 1951 book *Successful Drawing*. Actually, let's bring in Ms. Cawlow for this. She's our art expert.

Ms. Cawlow: Okay.

Prof. Barry: Have you ever heard of Loomis, Ms. Cawlow?

Ms. Cawlow: Yeah. He has a whole series of art books, right?

Prof. Barry: Yup. One's called *Fun with a Pencil*. Another is called *The Eye of the Painter*. He's also got one about drawing heads and hands.

Ms. Cawlow: I've read *Fun with a Pencil*.

Prof. Barry: Good. In all his books, he tries to demystify drawing and help people understand that there are certain knowable methods and mechanics that can make the whole process a little easier.

Here's a useful question he asks in *Successful Drawing*. I think it also applies to successful writing.

Ms. Cawlow: "Since the knowledge is available, why try to struggle along without it?"

Prof. Barry: And here's his follow-up sentence.

Ms. Cawlow: "The difficulties of not knowing are always much greater than the effort of learning."

Prof. Barry: Isn't that pretty good?

Yes, learning to write is hard work. Yes, learning to write is time-consuming and full of setbacks. But just imagine the obstacles you'll face if you never figure out how to do it. How will you communicate effectively at work? How will you communicate effectively with your friends and family? How will you put down on paper—or even in an email—the thoughts you deem important?

Cover letters, thank-you cards, grant proposals, tweets: think of all the ways in which writing enters and influences your life. You'll be at a real disadvantage, both professionally and personally, if you never learn how to do it properly. You'll also miss out on an inner freedom that comes with being able to fill up a blank page with your ideas and observations. The writer Susan Sontag describes that freedom in the following way.

Ms. Cawlow: "Writing is finally a series of permissions you give yourself to be expressive in certain ways. To invent. To leap. To fly. To fall. To find your own characteristic way of narrating and insisting."

Prof. Barry: The title of the essay that statement appears in, "Writing as Reading," gives us a nice stopping point for class today. It usefully recalls a connection we made all the way back at the beginning of our discussion today: the connection between writing and reading.

Read our motto for us one more time, Ms. Cawlow.

Ms. Cawlow: "To write good sentences, you need to read good sentences."

Prof. Barry: Exactly. To write good sentences, you need to read good sentences. We'll want to keep that in mind next class as well, when we look at examples involving everything from an Uber ad, to the Declaration of Independence, to a "Keep Out" sign in Scooba, Mississippi.

Our goal is to understand how these examples and many other catchy constructions make use of what is consistently the favorite writing technique of students who take my courses: the Rule of Three.

See you then.

Notes

Chapter 1

2 **"casual or cursory"** *Peruse*, MERRIAM-WEBSTER, https://www.merriam-webster.com/dictionary/peruse (last visited Apr. 30, 2019).

3 **"life of the law"** Oliver Wendell Holmes Jr., THE COMMON LAW 1 (1881; repr., 1991).

4 **"An advocate needs to advocate"** There are a bunch of examples of fun heteronymic sentences. Google the term. You're bound to find something. Perhaps you'll even craft a few of your own. Here are two more that made me smile, if somewhat cringingly: (1) "In the morning, we'll go fishing for bass. And on our way there, because I got new speakers, we'll pump the bass." (2) "You might hope that a mobile home in Mobile, Alabama, has, over the crib, a mobile for the baby."

Chapter 3

11 **"more myth than reality"** Mark Ribowsky, JOSH GIBSON: THE POWER AND THE DARKNESS 41–42 (2004).

11 **"held by Ty Cobb"** Ty Cobb, Al Stump & Charles C. Alexander, MY LIFE IN BASEBALL: THE TRUE RECORD (1993); Charles Leerhsen, TY COBB: A TERRIBLE BEAUTY (2016).

12 **"ruled it a home run"** Robert Peterson, ONLY THE BALL WAS WHITE: A HISTORY OF LEGENDARY BLACK PLAYERS AND ALL-BLACK PROFESSIONAL TEAMS 158 (1992).

12 **"yesterday, in Pittsburgh"** *Id.*

Chapter 4

14 **"John F. Kennedy came to the University of Michigan"** *The Founding Moment*, PEACE CORPS, https://www.peacecorps.gov/about/history/founding-moment/ (last visited Apr. 30, 2019).

16 **"accompanied Jacqueline Kennedy to Paris"** *News Conference 12, June 2, 1961*, JOHN F. KENNEDY PRESIDENTIAL LIBR. & MUSEUM, https://www.jfklibrary.org/archives/other-resources/john-f-kennedy-press-conferences/news-conference-12 (last visited Apr. 30, 2019).

18 **"living as an artist"** James Joyce, A Portrait of the Artist as a Young Man 166 (1916; repr., 2001).

Chapter 5

19 **"the winner says it may be difficult, but it's possible"** Lawrence W. Reed, *Althea Gibson: A Winning Attitude*, Found. for Econ. Educ., Oct. 9, 2015, https://fee.org/articles/the-winner-always-has-a-program/.

19 **"because you stop running"** Christopher McDougall, Born to Run 98 (2009).

21 **"harassing the printer"** Sam Slote, Ulysses in the Plural: The Variable Editions of Joyce's Novel 4 (2004), https://www.academia.edu/2531525/Ulysses_in_the_Plural_The_Variable_Editions_of_Joyces_Novel.

21 **"Stephen King"** In King's version of the story, Joyce "indicated assent without even raising his head to look at the friend." Stephen King, On Writing: A Memoir of the Craft 146 (2000). But the early readers of this book said that expressing Joyce's assent in words would be easier to follow, so I went with that.

Chapter 6

24 **"had muscles"** Cate Reynolds, *Some of Baseball's Most Prolific Hitters Called Maryland's Eastern Shore Home*, What's Up? Media, Apr. 3, 2015, https://whatsupmag.com/news/baseball-s-prolific-hitters-called-maryland-s-eastern-shore-home/.

24 **"in his hair"** *Jimmie Foxx*, New World Encyclopedia, https://www.newworldencyclopedia.org/entry/Jimmie_Foxx (last visited Apr. 30, 2019).

Chapter 7

26 **"World War II"** Ben Bradlee Jr., The Kid: The Immortal Life of Ted Williams 221–45 (2013).

26 **"second stint of service"** *Id.* at 335–36.

28 **"greatest hitter who ever lived"** Ted Williams & John Underwood, My Turn at Bat: The Story of My Life 7 (1988).

30 **"read good writing"** *Chief Justice John G. Roberts Jr.*, Scribes J.L. Writing, 2010, at 5.

30 **"reading good prose"** Bryan A. Garner, Garner on Language and Writing 16 (2009).

31 **"taking it apart"** Annie Dillard, The Writing Life 36 (2013).

Chapter 9

36 **"safely to the earth"** President John F. Kennedy, Special Message to the Congress on Urgent National Needs (May 25, 1961), https://www.nasa.gov/vision/space/features/jfk_speech_text.html.

Chapter 10

40 **"one thousand theories"** Thomas L. Friedman, The World Is Flat: A Brief History of the Twenty-First Century 414 (2005).

41 **"learn a hundred times"** Oliver Sacks, On the Move: A Life 173 n.2 (2015).

42 **"individual patients"** *Id.* at 173.

Chapter 11

44 **"Learning from Chekhov"** Francine Prose, *Chapter 10: Learning from Chekhov, in* Reading like a Writer: A Guide for People Who Love Books and for Those Who Want to Write Them 233 (2012).

44 **"great website"** *See* Quote Investigator, https://quoteinvestigator.com/ (last visited Apr. 30, 2019).

45 **"face a crisis"** The Country Girl (Pearlberg-Seaton Productions 1955).

46 **"rolled past like a ball"** Anton Chekhov, The Unknown Chekhov: Stories and Other Writings of Anton Chekhov Hitherto Unpublished 14 (Avrahm Yarmolinsky trans., 1954).

Chapter 12

48 **"concrete to the general and back"** Philip Lopate, To Show and To Tell: The Craft of Literary Nonfiction 53 (2013).

Chapter 13

51 **"a war"** Virginia Woolf, *Part Two: Time Passes, in* To the Lighthouse 125–44 (1927; repr., 1994).

Chapter 14

55 **"no way anybody will ever watch"** James Andrew Miller & Tom Shales, Those Guys Have All the Fun: Inside the World of ESPN 19 (2011).

55 **"about the future"** *It's Difficult to Make Predictions, Especially about the Future*, Quote Investigator (Oct. 20, 2013), https://quoteinvestigator.com/2013/10/20/no-predict/.

Chapter 16

59 **"tossed his glove"** George Plimpton, *Ernest Hemingway: The Art of Fiction No. 21*, Paris Rev., Spring 1958.

61 **"dirty floor"** This quote can be easily found on the internet, but I have been unable to connect it to one of Oates's specific works. It is usually cited with

only an attribution to her name. A possible origin comes from an oral interview Oates gave more than thirty years ago. *See* Helen Trinca, *Creatures of Habit Revealed in Mason Currey's Book "Daily Rituals,"* Australian (Nov. 2, 2013) ("Joyce Carol Oates is one of the most prolific modern writers but in 1987 told an interviewer that 'getting the first draft finished is like pushing a peanut with your nose across a very dirty floor'").

Chapter 18

66 **"Revision is reading again and again"** Michael Eric Dyson, What Truth Sounds Like 164 (2018).

68 **"not limited to sight alone"** One of my law students, Stephen Rees, said that this point about moving beyond the sense of sight reminded him of season 7, episode 2 of *Game of Thrones*, where the character Arya asks for more specific details about her enemies: "What do they look like? What do they smell like? How do they move? How hard are they to kill?" I plan to steal this great example for a future teaching opportunity.

68 **"burning house"** Sonia Sotomayor, My Beloved World 270 (2013).

68 **"cold blade"** *Id.* at 269.

69 **"make a story real"** *Id.* at 270.

Chapter 19

70 **"image and noise"** Mary Karr, The Art of Memoir 71 (2015).

70 **"brim over"** *Id.*

71 **"argues for its truth"** *Id.* at 72.

72 **"I can picture"** John Updike, More Matter: Essays and Criticism 182 (1999).

Chapter 20

73 **"smooth as butternut"** John Updike, *Hub Fans Bid Kid Adieu*, New Yorker (Oct. 22, 1960), https://www.newyorker.com/magazine/1960/10/22/hub-fans-bid-kid-adieu.

74 **"sweat in your eyebrows"** John Updike, Rabbit, Run 5 (1960).

74 **"looks the other way"** John Updike, Rabbit Redux 272–73 (1971).

Chapter 21

76 **"miniature golf"** John Updike, Golf Dreams 138 (1996).

77 **"any pitch"** For a look into Crane's interest in—indeed, obsession with—baseball, *see* John Berryman, Stephen Crane: A Critical Biography 12–24 (1950); *see also* Jacob Gedetsis, *Baseball, Experiences at SU Influence Author Stephen Crane*, Daily Orange (Feb. 10, 2015), http://dailyorange.com/2015/02/baseball-experiences-at-su-influence-author-stephen-crane/.

77 **"1960 Olympic team"** Scott F. Parker ed., CONVERSATIONS WITH KEN KESEY 24–25 (2014); *see also Ken Kesey on Misconceptions of Counterculture*, NPR (Aug. 12, 2011), https://www.npr.org/2011/08/12/139259106/ken-kesey-on-misconceptions-of-counterculture.

78 **"shake off one world"** Adam Begley, *Don DeLillo: The Art of Fiction No. 135*, PARIS REV., Fall 1993.

78 **"Running!"** Joyce Carol Oates, *To Invigorate Literary Mind, Start Moving Literary Feet*, N.Y. TIMES (July 19, 1999), https://www.nytimes.com/1999/07/19/arts/to-invigorate-literary-mind-start-moving-literary-feet.html.

78 **"reason most people run"** Haruki Murakami, WHAT I TALK ABOUT WHEN I TALK ABOUT RUNNING: A MEMOIR 80 (2009).

79 **"helps you to do that"** *Id.* at 80–81.

79 **"Exerting yourself"** *Id.* at 80.

Chapter 22

80 **"didn't like sports"** David Sedaris, *Go Carolina*, *in* ME TALK PRETTY ONE DAY 3, 5 (2000).

80 **"hated sports"** John Green, LOOKING FOR ALASKA 45 (2005).

82 **"his Fitbit"** David Sedaris, *Stepping Out*, NEW YORKER (June 23, 2014), https://www.newyorker.com/magazine/2014/06/30/stepping-out-3.

82 **"begin to flow"** Journal Entry by Henry David Thoreau (July 12, 1851), *Thoreau's Journal* (Part IV), ATLANTIC, Apr. 1905, https://www.theatlantic.com/magazine/archive/1905/04/thoreaus-journal-part-iv/542109/.

82 **"dull to read"** *Id.*

Chapter 23

84 **"genocide"** Steven Pinker, THE BETTER ANGELS OF OUR NATURE: WHY VIOLENCE HAS DECLINED 326 (2011).

85 **"hundreds of thousands"** David Livingstone Smith, LESS THAN HUMAN: WHY WE DEMEAN, ENSLAVE, AND EXTERMINATE OTHERS 14 (2011).

85 **"a few of the survivors"** *Id.*

85 **"worse than animals"** *Id.*

85 **"Irish Catholics"** Pinker, BETTER ANGELS 326.

86 **"nit would make a louse"** *Id.*

86 **"Nits make lice"** *Id.*

87 **"circle of sympathy"** *Id.* at xxvi.

88 **"human rights"** *Id.* at 176.

88 **"18th century"** *Id.* at 177.

88 **"change in policy"** *Id.*

91 **"moral center"** For a more critical assessment of Atticus Finch, *see* Malcolm Gladwell, *The Courthouse Ring*, NEW YORKER (Aug. 3, 2009), https://www.newyorker.com/magazine/2009/08/10/the-courthouse-ring.

Chapter 24

92 **"book of great power and courage"** Bryan Stevenson, Just Mercy: A Story of Justice and Redemption (2015).

Chapter 25

94 **"Dogon dress"** Binyavanga Wainaina, *How to Write about Africa*, Granta (Jan. 19, 2006), https://granta.com/how-to-write-about-africa/.

94 **"bogged down"** *Id.*

95 **"unparticular"** *Id.*

96 **"more than two decades"** Amy McDonald, *Uncola: Seven-Up, Counterculture and the Making of an American Brand*, Duke Univ. Libr.: Devil's Tale (Dec. 4, 2017), https://blogs.library.duke.edu/rubenstein/2017/12/04/uncola/.

96 **"T-Mobile"** *About T-Mobile*, T-Mobile.com, https://www.t-mobile.com/our-story/uncarrier-history (last visited Apr. 30, 2019).

96 **"typical Hardy usage"** Alan Bennett, The History Boys 55 (2004).

97 **"unslaved"** Colum McCann, TransAtlantic 284 (2013).

97 **"curious and lovely word"** *Id.*

Chapter 26

98 **"host of the *Daily Show*"** You Laugh but It's True (Day 1 Films 2012).

Chapter 27

101 **"America's Mandela"** Nicholas Kristof, *When Whites Just Don't Get It, Part 3*, N.Y. Times (Oct. 11, 2014), https://www.nytimes.com/2014/10/12/opinion/sunday/nicholas-kristof-when-whites-just-dont-get-it-part-3.html.

101 **"courage and conviction"** Bryan Stevenson, Just Mercy: A Story of Justice and Redemption inside flap (2014).

101 **"worst thing we've ever done"** *Id.* at 17–18.

102 **"disconnected from my own"** *Id.* at 289.

102 **"shared brokenness"** *Id.*

102 **"poverty in the South Bronx"** Adrian Nicole LeBlanc, Random Family: Love, Drugs, Trouble, and Coming of Age in the Bronx (2003).

102 **"homeless children"** Andrea Elliot, *Invisible Child*, N.Y. Times (Dec. 9, 2013), http://www.nytimes.com/projects/2013/invisible-child/index.html#/?chapt=1.

Chapter 30

108 **"rebellious roar"** Tom Peterkin, *Awful Author Addicted to Alliteration Achieves Acclaim Again*, Telegraph (Sept. 18, 2006), https://www.telegraph.co.uk/news/uknews/1529100/Awful-author-addicted-to-alliteration-achieves-acclaim-again.html.

108 **"Uniquely dreadful"** Miles Corwin, *Words to Remember*, SMITHSONIAN MAG. (June 2009, citing the *Oxford Companion to Irish Literature*), https://www.smithsonianmag.com/arts-culture/words-to-remember-133116350/.
109 **"Stephen King"** Stephen King, ON WRITING: A MEMOIR OF THE CRAFT 213 (2010).
109 **"Kill your darlings"** *Id.* at 222.
109 **"uninterested in readers"** Ben Yagoda, THE SOUND ON THE PAGE 97 (2004).

Chapter 31

113 **"closer to $24 billion"** Anthony Flint, *10 Years Later, Did the Big Dig Deliver?*, BOS. GLOBE (Dec. 29, 2015), https://www.bostonglobe.com/magazine/2015/12/29/years-later-did-big-dig-deliver/tSb8PIMS4QJUETsMpA7SpI/story.html.

Chapter 32

115 **"I love deadlines"** Douglas Adams, THE SALMON OF DOUBT: HITCHHIKING THE GALAXY ONE LAST TIME xxiii (2002).

Chapter 33

116 **"chocolate we eat"** Bridgette Carr et al., HUMAN TRAFFICKING LAW AND POLICY x (2014).

Chapter 36

124 **"virtuoso practicing scales"** Chad Harbach, THE ART OF FIELDING 5 (2011).
125 **"almost medical"** Jeffrey Eugenides, THE MARRIAGE PLOT 7 (2011).
125 **"almost scientifically"** Karen Armstrong, THE CASE FOR GOD 150 (2009).
125 **"almost cadaverous"** Siddhartha Mukherjee, THE GENE: AN INTIMATE HISTORY 278 (2016).
126 **"even sexy"** Roddy Doyle, THE DEPORTEES AND OTHER STORIES 4 (2007).
126 **"even treasuring"** Alice Munro, TOO MUCH HAPPINESS (2009).
126 **"even contradictory"** T. J. Stiles, THE FIRST TYCOON: THE EPIC LIFE OF CORNELIUS VANDERBILT 5 (2009).
127 **"even a noble"** Mark Twain, PUNCH, BROTHERS, PUNCH (1876), repr. in *Punch, Brothers, Punch*, LITERATURE NETWORK, http://www.online-literature.com/twain/3268/ (last visited Apr. 30, 2019).
127 **"even anxious"** Mark Twain, THE $30,000 BEQUEST (1906), repr. in *The $30,000 Bequest*, AM. LITERATURE, https://americanliterature.com/author/mark-twain/short-story/the-30000-bequest (last visited Apr. 30, 2019).
128 **"Since the knowledge is available"** Andrew Loomis, SUCCESSFUL DRAWING 29 (1951).
128 **"difficulties of not knowing"** *Id.*
128 **"To invent. To leap."** Susan Sontag, WHERE THE STRESS FALLS 263 (2001).

Photo Credits

Chapter 1

"Justice Oliver Wendell Holmes." National Photo Company. Available in the public domain. https://commons.wikimedia.org/wiki/File:Justice_Oliver_Wendell_Holmes_at_desk.jpg.

Smith, John Matthew. "Berry Gordy, Founder of Motown Records, March 12, 1998." NABOB, Washington, DC. Licensed under CC BY-SA. https://commons.wikimedia.org/wiki/File:Berry_Gordy.jpg.

Chapter 3

"Josh Gibson." Harrison Studio. Available in the public domain. https://commons.wikimedia.org/wiki/File:Josh_Gibson_1931.jpg.

Chapter 4

Thompson, Paul. "Babe Ruth." Available in the public domain. https://commons.wikimedia.org/wiki/File:Babe_Ruth_by_Paul_Thompson,_1920.jpg.

Stanger, Eck. "John F. Kennedy on the Michigan Union Steps—Peace Corps Speech." Licensed under CC-BY. https://quod.lib.umich.edu/b/bhl/x-bl000107/BL000107?bbdbid=14061;lasttype=bbaglist;lastview=bbthumbnail;resnum=28;size=100;start=1;subview=detail;view=bbentry;xc=1.

Knudsen, Robert. "Mrs. Kennedy in the Diplomatic Reception Room, 5 December 1961, White House, Diplomatic Reception Room." Available in the public domain. https://commons.wikimedia.org/wiki/File:Mrs._Kennedy_in_the_Diplomatic_Reception_Room_(cropped).jpg.

"I Voted for Betty's Husband." Courtesy of Gerald R. Ford Museum.

Ehrenzweig, Alex. "James Joyce, 1915." Available in the public domain. https://commons.wikimedia.org/wiki/File:James_Joyce_by_Alex_Ehrenzweig,_1915.jpg.

Chapter 6

"George Orwell Press Photo." Branch of the National Union of Journalists. Available in the public domain. https://commons.wikimedia.org/wiki/File:George_Orwell_press_photo.jpg.

"Jimmie Foxx of the Boston Red Sox." Harris & Ewing, 1937 All-Stars, Washington, DC. Available in the public domain. https://commons.wikimedia.org/wiki/File:Jimmie_Foxx_1937_cropped.jpg.

"1939 Ted Williams." Apex Photo Company. Available in the public domain. https://commons.wikimedia.org/wiki/File:1939_Ted_Williams.png.

Chapter 7

"Ted Williams Swearing into the Navy, 1942." US government. Available in the public domain. https://commons.wikimedia.org/wiki/File:Ted_Williams_swearing_into_the_Navy_1942.jpg.

"Official Portrait of John Glenn." US Senate Historical Office. Available in the public domain. https://commons.wikimedia.org/wiki/File:John_Glenn_Low_Res.jpg.

Gottlieb, William P. "Portrait of Charlie Parker in 1947." Available in the public domain. https://commons.wikimedia.org/wiki/File:Portrait_of_Charlie_Parker_in_1947.jpg.

Nadar, Félix. "Édouard Manet." Available in the public domain. https://commons.wikimedia.org/wiki/File:F%C3%A9lix_Nadar_1820-1910_portraits_Edouard_Manet.jpg.

Petteway, Steve. "Chief Justice John G. Roberts." Available in the public domain. https://commons.wikimedia.org/wiki/File:Official_roberts_CJ.jpg.

Easterbrook, Frank H. "Judge Easterbrook." Available in the public domain. https://en.wikipedia.org/wiki/Frank_H._Easterbrook#/media/File:JudgeEasterbrook.JPG.

Chapter 8

Jewell, Alden. "Rolls-Royce Silver Cloud, 1959." Licensed under CC BY 2.0. https://www.flickr.com/photos/autohistorian/46293728372.

"John F. Kennedy, President of the United States." White House Press Office. Available in the public domain. https://commons.wikimedia.org/wiki/File:John_F._Kennedy,_White_House_photo_portrait,_looking_up.jpg.

Chapter 9

"Kennedy Giving Historic Speech to Congress." NASA. Available in the public domain. https://commons.wikimedia.org/wiki/File:Kennedy_Giving_Historic_Speech_to_Congress_-_GPN-2000-001658.jpg.

Chapter 10

"Official Portrait of President Ronald Reagan." Available in the public domain. https://en.wikipedia.org/wiki/File:Official_Portrait_of_President_Reagan_1981.jpg.

"Ronald Reagan Speaking in Front of the Brandenburg Gate and the Berlin Wall on June 12, 1987." White House Photographic Office. Available in the public domain. https://sco.wikipedia.org/wiki/File:ReaganBerlinWall.jpg.

"William Carlos Williams." Beinecke Rare Book and Manuscript Library, Yale University. Available in the public domain. https://commons.wikimedia.org/wiki/Category:William_Carlos_Williams#/media/File:William_Carlos_Williams_passport_photograph_1921.jpg.

"Anton Chekhov in Yalta, 1900." Available in the public domain. https://en.wikipedia.org/wiki/Anton_Chekhov#/media/File:Anton_Chekhov_with_bow-tie_sepia_image.jpg.

Chapter 12

Vartdal, Andreas. "Alice Munro." Licensed under CC BY-SA. https://commons.wikimedia.org/wiki/File:Alice_Munro_teikna_av_Andreas_Vartdal_(cc-by-sa).jpg.

Chapter 15

Thomas, C. "Monica Seles, U.S. Hardcourt Finals, San Antonio, 1991." Licensed under CC BY 2.0. https://commons.wikimedia.org/wiki/File:Monica_Seles_1991.jpg.

Chapter 16

Arnold, Lloyd. "Hemingway Posing for a Dust Jacket Photo for the First Edition of *For Whom the Bell Tolls*, at the Sun Valley Lodge, Idaho, Late 1939." Available in the public domain. https://commons.wikimedia.org/wiki/File:ErnestHemingway.jpg.

Van Vechten, Carl. "Portrait of Boxer Joe Louis." Available in the public domain. https://commons.wikimedia.org/wiki/File:Joe_Louis_by_van_Vechten.jpg.

Chapter 18

Petteway, Steve. "Sonia Sotomayor, U.S. Supreme Court Justice." Available in the public domain. https://en.wikipedia.org/wiki/File:Sonia_Sotomayor_in_SCOTUS_robe.jpg.

Chapter 19

"John Updike with Bushes." George Bush Presidential Library. Available in the public domain. https://commons.wikimedia.org/wiki/File:John_Updike_with_Bushes.jpg.

Chapter 21

"American Author Stephen Crane in 1989." Available in the public domain. https://commons.wikimedia.org/wiki/File:StephenCrane1899.jpg.

Chapter 23

Brady, Mathew. "Lyman Beecher." Available in the public domain. https://commons.wikimedia.org/wiki/File:Lyman_Beecher_-_Brady-Handy.jpg.

"Gregory Peck Atticus Finch Publicity Photo." Universal Pictures. Available in the public domain. https://commons.wikimedia.org/wiki/File:Gregory_Peck_Atticus_Finch_Publicity_Photo.jpg.

Chapter 27

"Nelson Mandela, 2000." Library of the London School of Economics and Political Science. Available in the public domain. https://commons.wikimedia.org/wiki/File:Nelson_Mandela,_2000_(5).jpg.

Chapter 29

"Portrait of Jane Austen, based on a portrait drawn by Cassandra Austen." Available in the public domain. https://commons.wikimedia.org/wiki/File:Jane_Austen.jpg.

Chapter 31

"Daniel Kahneman." US government. Available in the public domain. https://commons.wikimedia.org/wiki/File:Daniel_KAHNEMAN.jpg.

"Boston CAT Project Construction View from Air." Available in the public domain. https://upload.wikimedia.org/wikipedia/commons/f/f7/Boston_CAT_Project-construction_view_from_air.jpeg.

Acknowledgments

One of the best parts of working on *The Syntax of Sports* series is that I get to collaborate with a team of wonderful people. Some of these people had already helped out with the first volume, *The Syntax of Sports, Class 1: Words Under the Words*. These include Tyler Berndt, Taylor Brook, Nick Cagle, Christina Cincilla, Becca Garfinkle, Michael Goldenberg, Myles Johnson, Akash Patel, Jose Peralta, Darien Perry, Scotti Petersen, Dimitra Rallis, Stephen Rees, André Rouillard, Gabrielle Sines, Kimiko Varner, Barb Vibbert, Sage Wen, and Justin Wooten. Others added usefully fresh eyes and ideas by joining the team for this new volume: Holly Clancy, Nick Dawson, Patrick Forte, Jack Igoe, Matt Preston, and Jack Ross.

All of them deserve extra praise for contributing excellent edits and feedback while also juggling the demands of a full load of other educational and professional pursuits. I really appreciate the many times they pushed "busyness to the corner," to borrow a phrase from Toni Morrison, so that sentences could be tightened, examples could be enlivened, and the overall reading experience of this book could be improved.

I am similarly grateful for the continued efforts of Jason Colman, Sean Guynes, Amanda Karby, and the rest of the group at Maize Books. It's been great to keep experiencing and learning from their innovative approach to publishing.

CPSIA information can be obtained
at www.ICGtesting.com
Printed in the USA
JSHW021233130221
11887JS00007B/53